PRODIGAL

PRODIGAL

DANIEL BURKHART

Ambassador International
Greenville, South Carolina & Belfast, Northern Ireland
www.ambassador-international.com

Prodigal

©2020 by Daniel Burkhart
All rights reserved

ISBN: 978-1-62020-678-2
eISBN: 978-1-62020-717-8

Cover Design and Page Layout by Hannah Nichols
eBook Conversion by Anna Riebe Raats
Edited By: Ann Hammitt

All rights reserved. No part of this book may be used or reproduced in any manner whatsoever without written permission except in the case of brief quotations embodied in critical articles or reviews.

Unless otherwise indicated, Bible quotations are taken from the King James Version, copyright © Cambridge University Press and Oxford University Press 1961, 1970. All rights reserved.

AMBASSADOR INTERNATIONAL
Emerald House
411 University Ridge, Suite B14
Greenville, SC 29601, USA
www.ambassador-international.com

AMBASSADOR BOOKS
The Mount
2 Woodstock Link
Belfast, BT6 8DD, Northern Ireland, UK
www.ambassadormedia.co.uk

The colophon is a trademark of Ambassador, a Christian publishing company.

*This book is dedicated to my loving and Godly mother,
Cecile M. Burkhart.
I love you, Mom, always and forever!*

CONTENTS

FOREWORD	9
PROLOGUE	13
PAW PAW	15
MIDDLE SCHOOL	19
HIGH SCHOOL	23
DESCENT FROM GRACE	31
THE FARMHOUSE	41
WHEN TRAGEDY STRIKES	49
THE BIRTH OF A MANAGER	57
THE PROMOTION	65
BAD DECISIONS	71
SUFFERING	85
ROAD TO REDEMPTION	93
CALIFORNIA DREAMS	99
NIGHTMARE	105
COMING HOME	117
GROWING PAINS	121
GIFT FROM GOD	127

THE HEART OF THE PROBLEM	133
OPENED DOOR	139
EPILOGUE	149

FOREWORD

WHEN I WOKE UP ON the morning of January 15, 2018, I never envisioned writing a book. In fact, the very process of having to edit a single chapter seemed too tedious and time consuming for me to sit still long enough to accomplish. It was a snowy morning outside of the rancher style house my wife and I live in, in the small quiet town of McConnellsburg, Pennsylvania. I thought I would be a good husband and go outside before my shift at work and clear off the snow from the driveway. We had just started a diet and I thought this would be a great opportunity to get some exercise along with added steps on my pedometer. As I shoveled the snow, I was thinking about my day ahead and what work was going to be like. I was gathering my thoughts for the day, not paying attention to the ice underneath the snow.

Suddenly, I slipped on a patch of ice. My left leg slid forward while my body fell backwards, my right leg folded underneath me. I will never forget the sound the top of my right knee made. The *pop* sounded almost like the crack of a baseball bat. The sound was followed by an intense pain.

I lay in the driveway wondering what I should do until my neighbor who was shoveling his own driveway at the time saw me and his wife called an ambulance. I came to find out that I had completely torn my quad from my kneecap.

I had surgery to repair the tear two days later and was then confined to a chair and an ottoman to rest my leg and keep ice on it. Since our bathroom was too narrow for me to hop into, my father-in-law graciously cut a hole in an old wooden dining room chair and placed a bucket underneath the hole. This make-shift commode sat directly across from my chair in the living room for the next eight weeks. It was extremely helpful and I appreciated it very much, but the smell was neither pleasant nor was it a welcoming sight for any visitors wanting to check in on me.

For the next eight weeks I tried to fill my time with activities that would challenge my brain. At first I tried to play the guitar. Allison, my wife, plays the guitar so we have a few in our house. I used YouTube as a means to take lessons that lasted about an hour and a half.

I decided to try to learn sign language. Allison also thought that was a good idea. For the next few weeks we would go through colors, basic questions, the letters of the alphabet, and numbers. It was very interesting and fun, but once we learned the basics I again got bored. I needed something else to occupy my time.

I finally grabbed my laptop and started to do some creative writing. The plan was to write a short story, since I had never written anything longer than a ten-page book report for college. Plans quickly changed once I started writing. An instant idea sprang in my head, *write your story*. That first day I wrote over twenty pages. I felt inspiration like I never have before.

During this process of healing for my knee, I asked God what it was that He wanted me to learn through this injury. I felt my mindset was right about the injury, but the purpose was hard to figure out. When I started writing the book, my purpose became crystal clear. For the next three weeks, from morning to evening I sat and wrote, pouring out my heart and giving an honest look into my life. Allison was my cheerleader—she encouraged me every day to finish the book. Finally, after three weeks I sat back and realized that what had started as a short story became an 82,000-word 254-page manuscript.

I hope that this story encourages, entertains, and enlightens you. I want to be very clear: I want to identify the sin and tough times in my life, but I do not want to glorify the sin. Though there are a lot of bad circumstances and problems that I faced throughout my journey, the key points of those moments are my mindset and the conviction I felt in the midst of these situations.

My goal is that the reader can see how easy bad decisions happen, how we justify them with our reasoning, and how even though people may look like they are having a great time, many people have an empty, hollow feeling living deep within them.

I also want the reader to take away from this story the love and forgiveness we have in our Heavenly Father. No matter who you are or what your background is, God loves you and wants you to be a part of His family. Once we are part of His family, we need to look at our relationship with Christ as a father-to-child relationship. This means we can serve the Lord out of love for Him, not out of a sense of obedience to your Master as a servant. The change in this dynamic is key for all Christians. I serve my Father because of my love for Him; I serve my boss due to a sense of fear of losing my job. My Father forgives me no matter what I have done; my boss will fire me if I do not do what he says. My Father yearns for a stronger, richer relationship and wants me to be successful, to have peace, and to have joy. My boss desires only for me to serve his purpose, my success in life is not his main concern for me. Obedience is his main concern for me.

God has always and will always be the same, we just need to see Him more clearly. I hope you enjoy this book, but more so, I hope it inspires you to have a deeper relationship with the Lord. No matter what your past is, God can give you a bright future. Enjoy *Prodigal* and be blessed.

Dan Burkhart
May 28, 2018

PROLOGUE

THE PARABLE, OR STORY, OF the prodigal son in Luke 15:11-32 is one most people hear as a child. The story begins with a rich man who had two sons: the oldest son was faithful to his father and would stay busy working in the fields tending to the crops, while his youngest son was curious of what the world would be like to explore and what adventures he had yet to experience. The father told his sons that when they were older he would give them their inheritance. His younger son, wanting to experience more of the world, came to his father and asked for his portion immediately instead of waiting. The father loved both of his sons very much and wanted them to be happy, so he gave the younger son his portion as the son had wished.

The younger son began his journey into life recklessly squandering his money on the new friends he had made and the sinful lifestyle he had acquired. He quickly lost all his riches and money and soon he was left with only the clothes he was wearing. All his friends disappeared once his money was gone. In order to live, he began to work for a farmer and took care of the swine. He was famished from hunger, even eating the slop for the pigs. He sat in the mud, miserable from the lifestyle and choices he had made. He thought that it would be better to be a servant in his father's house than to eat the slop with these beasts. He thought that if he went back to his father and begged for forgiveness his father would grant him this wish.

The younger son embarked on the long journey back to his family. He smelled of pigs and his clothes were dirty and tattered. The rich man looked out from his fields and saw someone coming toward his house. When the father realized it was his prodigal son, he ran to meet him. The younger son begged his father for forgiveness and asked him if he could be a servant for his father. The son was willing to live in the servants' quarters and not be considered part of his family anymore. The father, hearing this, replied, "My son who was once lost is now found. He was once dead but is now alive." The father had his servants take the younger son and bathe him. They clothed him in the finest apparel and prepared a feast to celebrate the return of the prodigal son.

PAW PAW

THE COURTHOUSE WAS PACKED WITH people weathered by drugs, bad decisions, hard living, and poverty. There was a musty smell, scattered with smoke residue. The faces of the young men and women waiting to be seen in front of the judge were docile and menacing. I sat outside waiting for my lawyer. I panicked because I had only enough money to pay for the fees of my court case, still having an incomplete payment to procure my lawyer. I smelled like Acqua Di Gio cologne littered with the lingering scent of the Newport cigarettes I had just chained smoked because of my nerves. I sat there in the midst of a crowd of unsettled souls, wearing a nice suit, while others wore faded jeans and t-shirts. My case was not for another hour, so as I sat trying not to worry, my mind wondered.

I thought back to a time when I didn't have a cigarette glued to my hand or money problems. My mind had to go a long way to reach it.

***

I did not have a tough childhood, in fact it was quite the opposite. My dad was the pastor of a church in West Virginia while mom was a substitute teacher at several schools in Cumberland to help earn extra income. I did not come from money, but what my family lacked in money, my parents made up for with their loving home. I was an only child. I had wished for brothers and sisters, but my parents were able to have only one child.

I grew up in the small town of Paw Paw, West Virginia. My dad, Ken, was the pastor of Paw Paw Bible Church. Standing six foot three inches tall, Ken had a commanding presence. His appearance reminded people of John

Goodman from *Roseanne*. He was a football player in high school and had scholarships to play for various Division I schools. My dad decided not to go to college for football, but instead to attend Washington Baptist College and become a pastor. He was boisterous and animated in his speech and was the life of any room he walked into. His personality was magnetic and I looked up to my father as my hero from a young age.

My mom, Cecilia, was French Canadian. She was born in Montreal, Quebec, and her first language was French. She moved to the United States at nine years old at which time she learned English. She lived in Ann Arbor, Michigan, with her family where she grew up. She was fluent in English and French, and although I never noticed her accent, others could tell. She was strong in her faith and also attended Bible college, where she met my dad. She had a humble demeanor about her—a gentle spirit. Mom was well liked by anyone who met her, as she let her love for the Lord and people shine bright.

My childhood home was a small house near the town library and a field where the kids gathered to play sports in the summer. Since I was an only child, I mostly kept to myself, and played downstairs in the basement with action figures. I had an active imagination and often daydreamed about being a wrestler or a superhero. I would put the pillows from the couch on the floor, climb on top, and pretend I was jumping off the top ropes of the ring. Every night my mom tucked me into bed and prayed with me. She told me even at a young age to pray for a wife someday and said God would send me the woman of my dreams if I prayed faithfully. I heard the barking of the neighbor's dog at night, so to drown out the sounds, Mom played cassette tapes of soft praise and worship songs. She told me that King David in the Bible used to be put to sleep by gently strumming a harp by his bed. My mom was my best friend growing up while my dad stayed extremely busy with the church.

I loved movies. There was a local video store that I went to with Mom and rented movies two to three times a week. I loved going into the video store in

Paw Paw and looking through the movies to discover an adventure. It was my favorite to get lost in the adventures of movies and to me, it was my escape from my boring life and a chance to be whatever I wanted to be. It was never a short trip to the video store since I always took an hour to go through all the cases until I found the movie cover that looked interesting.

Soon after my third-grade year, my dad told my mom and me that God was leading him to teach teenagers how to evangelize and disciple others in Martinsburg, West Virginia. The previous director had worked with my dad and challenged him to take over for her. She had recently passed away and the next morning, Dad felt God leading him to work as the director in Child Evangelism Fellowship. I did not understand what that meant, but I loved the fact that I would be moving to a bigger town with more than one convenient store and one restaurant. I had made a lot of friendships with my classmates, but this next step in life brought about a lot of excitement. Moving day arrived and we moved our things to our new home.

During the summer, I tagged along with Mom and Dad as they ministered. My dad, with his new position, would work as the director for over eight counties for Child Evangelism Fellowship. They trained teenagers that were willing to learn how to teach Bible lessons and missionary stories. I was the practice student for these teenagers. I enjoyed hearing the different types of storytelling methods the teens used. I often practiced telling the stories to Mom and Dad, telling it better than most of the students because I took everyone's stories and combined them into the best version. I have an eidetic memory that helps me remember even the smallest details of every encounter that occurs.

In the new house in Martinsburg, my bedroom was to the right of the top of the stairs and it was great except for one feature—the door to the attic was in my room. It was scary hearing all the creaks and sounds of the attic at night. I slept with a night light globe of the world and music on smooth jazz to calm me down and take my mind off the sounds of the wind going through the attic. Eventually my parents remodeled the attic and it became an office for mom. Many nights she was in the office late, but I did not mind the late nights because I had the security of knowing she was there.

MIDDLE SCHOOL

RIGHT BEFORE GOING INTO MIDDLE school, I went on a trip to Michigan with my parents to visit mom's family during the summer. All Mom's side of the family still resided in Ann Arbor. While we were there, we went to the mall with Mom's brother, my Uncle Joe. Uncle Joe was successful and had two daughters much older than me. Uncle Joe needed to buy my cousins a Starter brand University of Michigan jackets. I was so enamored by the size of the mall that I did not pay much attention to what was going on. Uncle Joe asked me to try on a jacket because I was about the same size as my cousins. The jacket fit well. Come to find out, Uncle Joe also bought me a Michigan jacket as a gift. That was the start of my love for the University of Michigan sports teams.

On the first day back from Michigan, I wore my Starter jacket to school, not knowing anything about the popularity of sports teams or the up-and-coming popularity of Starter as a brand. I quickly learned when some of the cool kids started asking me about the jacket and about why I liked Michigan. I wanted to fit in so I told them I loved Michigan. I started cheering on Michigan and the group of players that were referred to as the "Fab Five" led by Chris Webber. I cheered them on throughout the entire NCAA tournament that year.

The rest of that school year seemed to fly by. While I made friends at school, when I got home it was just me and my parents. My escape was in movies, television shows, and books. Boredom had become my common companion. When Mom and Dad were away with their ministry either visiting another church or working at children camps, I stayed with my grandparents in their house about ten to twelve miles from ours. My grandma was a sweet, talkative older woman who was very loving and compassionate to all who she met. My grandpa was the hardest worker I knew. He spent most of the days working at an automobile parts factory, then worked late into the evening on his farm. He had a quiet demeanor about him but I knew to behave because I did not want him to pull out the paddle. Times at my grandparents' house were far less boring and I spent hours talking with my grandma and even went on walks with her after dinner. I loved the time I spent with grandma because she was so friendly and easy to talk with.

Just like every Christmas, I went with my parents to my grandparents' house to exchange gifts and eat my grandma's amazing cooking. That year, my grandparents got me something that proved to help me not only pass the time, but also brought about a means to stay out of trouble through my entire middle and high school years—a basketball hoop and basketball.

Every day after school I dropped off my backpack, picked up my basketball, and shot hoops until dinner. I spent hours outside shooting hoops and imagining myself as a part of the Michigan basketball program. I lost myself in basketball and it quickly turned into my biggest passion. Dad came outside and threw the ball against the backboard and I grabbed the rebound and put the ball back to score. I loved those times with Dad, but as the years went on, those times became few and far between.

I spent every free moment I had playing basketball and listening to music. I wished for a friend to play against—I got lonely shooting around by myself. Mom suggested that I pray for God to send me a friend. I made this prayer request for several weeks. One day, a church member invited me to play basketball with him and some others. I went and met Derrick—a friend that would prove to be invaluable for years to come. Derrick was tall and lean and the same age as me. We played one-on-one basketball that day after the older boys left. Even though I was tall, I was chubby and slow. Every time

I went to check the ball to Derrick, I threw the ball away from Derrick so he had to run to get it. I wanted my tactic to wear Derrick out, leveling the playing field. Of course, Derrick caught on to what I was doing and retaliated by doing the same thing. I quickly became exhausted. I lost several games in a row to Derrick, but that day started a friendship that carried through the rest of my life.

Now every day after school, I called Derrick up and we met at the local elementary school to play basketball together. We were inseparable. Since Derrick was homeschooled, it felt like I had a secret friend that I discovered and got to hang out with after school. Derrick asked me what it was like to go to a real school and I found out what it was like to do schoolwork at home and have the rest of the day to play and hang out. We searched for loose change lying around the house and played for HOKO's, a cold chocolate drink, at the vending machine by the fire hall located near my house. When we played at the school we bet on sodas and Doritos since there was a convenient store near the school. Most of the time I lost, but the times I won I felt like a king.

During my last year in middle school, I became a very talkative guy. To fit in, I often said inappropriate comments to get the rest of the kids to laugh. I felt bad about this in my heart because of my faith; I felt trapped in an internal battle. Throughout the entire year, my struggle between my faith in God and my longing to be popular wore on. I realized that if I was going to be in high school with these same people, I would end up not just conforming to the popular standard over my faith, but that peer pressure might lead to drinking and possibly drugs. I did not want to hurt my parents in this way. I asked my parents if I could go to a Christian school. I knew that I would be surrounded by people who could help me grow in my faith and love for God. In the summer after my eighth-grade year, I enrolled in Mercy Academy.

HIGH SCHOOL

THE HARD, COLD WOOD OF the bench in the courtroom foyer made me feel anxious and clammy. My imagination raced as I sat waiting. "Will my lawyer show up?" I thought to myself. I wished that my life was a movie, maybe *Back to the Future*. I hoped that Doc Brown would zoom up to the front of the courtroom in a 1982 model DeLorean yelling for me to come out and jump in. These random, obscure thoughts were all that could keep me calm. If I could time travel just once, I would be able to change the trajectory of my life.

* * *

I began the new school year at Mercy Academy optimistic about fitting in and enjoying my new school. My freshman year was exactly what I had hoped. Mercy's basketball team had many openings, so there was good opportunity for me to make the varsity team as a freshman. During the day I studied the Bible and my other subjects, then in the evenings I hung out with Derrick. The first day of basketball tryouts came and I was nervous. I had not expected so much running and endurance training. For the first two weeks they barely picked up a basketball. I was out of shape and overweight. The coach was an older man who was filled with pride about the teams he had coached in the past and when he saw my height, all he could focus on was trying to motivate me to lose weight. I was used to being made fun of because of my weight by my peers, but I had never been ridiculed by a grown adult. I felt targeted, but I had never been on an organized team, so I thought this was normal. Although I was out of shape, I tried as hard as I could and worked both during practice and after school to better my endurance and skills. I was excited when I found out that I had made the team as a freshman playing for a varsity squad, even if I was just a benchwarmer.

One of my new friends that came to Mercy Academy that year was Rick. Rick also played basketball. He wasn't very coordinated, but his height gave him an intimidation factor. Rick was older than me even though we were in the same grade, so Rick could drive. He came over to my house and we played basketball with Derrick. All three of us hung out often. Rick reminded me of the friends I had in middle school. Rick liked to joke around, and he wasn't the best of influences. I remember one time I got in trouble for dropping Rick's shorts in the foyer of the gym after school. We did that to each other in the locker room, but I thought I would try to get Rick when he was around girls. I got a bad reputation as a troublemaker and I didn't like it. Around this time, Mom often told me that I was not stupid but that I just did dumb things.

Basketball season quickly arrived and I was a starter. I had worked hard on my conditioning and even though I was still heavyset, I had lost a good amount of weight. I was still hearing it from the coach even though I had a breakout year. My team started out with a victory, already beating the previous year's record. Five games into the season Mercy had a comeback victory where I scored twenty-four points and twenty-one rebounds. I was on my way to a great season as a sophomore, but things were about to take a drastic turn for the worst.

First, two of the starters' grades became too low to play, so they were no longer on the team. Then Coach Rollins, out of frustration, blamed me for their inability to win more games. He made comments about my weight and made fun of me openly around the rest of the team. Coach Rollins benched me for the majority of games the rest of the year. I became frustrated and depressed. I loved basketball and just wanted the opportunity to play.

Dad taught in Christian schools with his ministry at the time. He established a strong relationship with the principal of one school in particular: Brethren Bible Christian Academy in Hagerstown. The principal just happened to be the head coach of the boys' basketball team. I asked Dad if I could transfer to BBCA after my sophomore year and Dad talked to the principal. Since my mom and dad both graduated from a college in Maryland, they could both substitute teach at BBCA to help the tuition cost. The plan to switch after the year ended was set in motion.

I looked forward to working with my parents' in the ministry that summer and getting ready for my final two years of high school at BBCA. I met with the principal since he was also my new basketball coach and I noticed a kindness and humility that was refreshing. During the meeting, Principal Williams told me about an assistant coach who had previously played with the Baltimore Bullets when they were in Baltimore several decades earlier. He said that if I wanted to, the assistant coach was willing to work three to four days a week during the summer with me to help me improve my physical fitness and overall skills. I jumped at the chance to train with him during the summer.

The first day of training came and I was excited and nervous. I arrived on time and was greeted by a tall man, bald and very friendly. Coach Stan Johnson was kind and had the same humility as Principal Williams. I started my training by stretching, then moved on to the conditioning exercises. Coach Johnson was patient with me and even helped me form the proper shooting technique. I no longer dreaded practice time—I looked forward to them, even counting those days as my favorite days of the week. I learned so much more than basketball from Coach Johnson. We discussed life issues and the wisdom Coach Johnson imparted was something that I looked forward to every week. Sometimes I brought Derrick along to learn, too. Some days I showed up for my practices and there were other teammates of mine working out with Coach Johnson. I built relationships with my new teammates and met my new classmates before I even started school. By the time summer ended, I had met a lot of new kids who would become my friends.

The first day of my new school arrived and Brethren Bible Christian Academy had the look of a normal high school. I learned that the teachers there carried themselves with a gentle and humble demeanor. I longed to learn this new attribute and I was thankful to God for helping me get away from the prideful atmosphere I was at previously. I always remembered what Mom had told me: "Pride comes before a fall and fall before destruction." Mom was wise beyond her years and always imparted wisdom from the Bible to me. She also noticed the loving kindness and gentle spirit that BBCA had. I loved the fact that my new school was diverse, and I enjoyed being able to attend a school with mixed races. This school year was going well, and I fit in better than I ever did at my old school. I loved all of my new classmates.

Basketball practices began and they were intense—the players were much better than that of my previous school. I knew if I was going to be a starter, I had to give it everything I had. My work ethic was strong and I practiced hard both at school and at home. Many days I was outside well into the night with only a street light and a flood light showing me the hoop. Even when it snowed, I shoveled the driveway and practiced my moves and foul shots outside. I never let any weather hold me down from my goals.

The feeling of anticipation for a new beginning fell upon me. At the first game of the season, the crowd was large and loud. I had worked so hard all summer long and throughout the year and it worked: I was picked as a starter. I averaged almost ten points and eleven rebounds that year. Many games even had a double-double. Best of all, I managed to build strong relationships with all the team members and coaching staff.

Derrick got his driver's license that year and started hanging with other friends as well as me. I began to hang out with Derrick's new friends and soon we became a clique. There was Marcus—he was the loud, outgoing one. He was a good-looking guy, tall with a sports build. He was not nervous or scared to talk to girls so he was the voice of the group. Then there was Jeff—he grew up homeschooled and was quiet, but extremely friendly and well-mannered. Jeff was the kindest and most considerate of all of those in the group. I loved hanging out with Derrick, Marcus, and Jeff—I had a group of people that were my close friends. That feeling of belonging was comforting to me. I was finally a senior, and I knew that my last year of high school was going to be a great one. But before my school year began, I helped my parents prepare the training camp we went to at the beginning of every summer for two weeks.

The camp was called "Camp Valley of Decisions." Though I had made a decision when I was young to accept Christ as my Savior, I still had a lot of doubts throughout my youth. My family believed in eternal security, which means that once you make the decision to accept Christ as your Savior, you are forever part of God's family. No sin you commit can take away the security of having Jesus in your heart. Though I fully believed this, I was aware that "the heart is deceitful above all things, and desperately wicked: who can know it? I the Lord search the heart, I try the reins." I constantly questioned whether I was a true Christian or not. Many nights during my personal prayer time I prayed the sinner's prayer and tried to reconfirm that I was indeed a Christian. It would become a struggle that I would carry for years.

One day as I played basketball with some of the other summer missionaries, I landed wrong from a layup and heard a pop in my foot. I couldn't put any pressure on my foot. Mom rushed me to the hospital and they found out that my foot was fractured. I was fitted with a cast and a pair of crutches. My first thought was despair. Was I going to be able to play basketball my senior year, or would this broken foot cause me to miss my biggest passion? The other challenge was getting to each of my summer classes while climbing hills at the campsite. Every day I hopped up the hills and back down to get to my classes. I already broke into a sweat just moving out of the air conditioning, but now I hopped through fields while being pestered by gnats and bugs in the high humidity of a West Virginia summer. Many times I came into class covered with sweat marks all over my shirt. Even though my fractured foot was inconvenient, I tried to view the hobbling and sweating as only another obstacle in my road to recovery. I used lessons I learned the previous summer from Coach Johnson as a way to keep myself laser-focused.

Through all the obstacles, I finished my two-week training. I headed home to tell Derrick what had happened. Even though I couldn't play basketball, I still went outside and hung out with Derrick. When the next doctor visit came, I found out I could walk around without my crutches. I went home and Derrick came over so we could shoot hoops. I moved around as normal, just with a booted cast on my foot. Derrick was excited because he had a growth spurt and was now able to dunk. Even though I was now six feet six inches tall, I barely touched the rim. One night after school I decided I would try to jump off my good leg and see if I could still touch the rim. To my surprise, I jumped up and my hand was almost completely over the metal. Apparently, all that jumping around on one leg up hills and long fields had strengthened my leg to the point that I could almost dunk. "This must be a fluke. I feel like the boy from *Rookie of the Year* who broke his arm and was suddenly able to throw 100 mph fastballs," I thought. I wanted to test my new ability at school to see if this was really happening, or if maybe the rim at my house was bent down. I went to meet Coach Johnson for a shooting practice during the summer, but there was no conditioning while I was recovering. As soon as I was in the gym, I went to the rim and jumped up and immediately grabbed the rim. I was excited because if I could get my cast off before the season, I would be able to add a new dynamic to my already skilled game.

My senior year started and I still wore my cast. I was supposed to get it off soon and to be on schedule to go to the first practice for basketball. Unfortunately, when the visit to the doctor came, the X-rays showed that my foot had not healed yet. The doctor told me that he thought that I would probably be missing this year's basketball season since my bone was healing slowly. I was completely discouraged. All of my dreams were shattered. Mom told me to pray that God would heal me in time for basketball season if it was His will. I thought that God was taking basketball away from me because it was taking the place of my time with God. I prayed almost any chance I got, asking God to let me heal and promised that if I was able to play, I would give all the glory to God.

The first day of basketball practice was one day away and Mom took me to the doctor. The doctor slowly drilled off the cast and did another X-ray on my foot. While waiting, Mom and I prayed that it was God's will to let me have a fully healed foot and be able to play this season. The doctor came back in the room with a look of wonder on his face. He told us that somehow my foot was fully healed and as long as I wore an ankle brace I could begin practice. Mom was so overwhelmed that she asked to have a word of prayer right there to thank God for letting me play. "I can't wait to go to school and tell the team the good news! Thank you, Lord!" I exclaimed. When I arrived to practice without a cast on my foot I was embraced immediately with a hug from the entire team. God had answered my prayer. That year was a personal best for me, and I gave all the glory to God, just as I had promised.

Like most years, that year was filled with highs and lows. We lost our star point guard the third game of the season for the rest of the year. I felt like I had to step up my game even more to help carry the burden for the team. We won a tournament later that year at Washington Baptist College on a buzzer beater by one of my closest friends and teammate, Manny. I scored sixteen points in the fourth quarter of that game and finished with twenty-four points and twenty rebounds.

The season was a success and I was named team MVP for the year at the awards ceremony. We finished with a winning record. I was so thankful to God for healing my foot and letting me play my senior year. I was starting to get letters from colleges to play for them, but most of the offers were for partial football scholarships, a sport not even offered at my school. I was named in the "Who's Who for High School Athletes" in a major college recruiting publication, so when colleges read my interests and size, they assumed I played football. My parents could not afford to send me to a big school unless I could get a full ride. I reluctantly applied to Washington Baptist College, where my mom and dad had met. I set up a visit to tour the campus at WBC with my parents.

Visiting day was full of potential students my age. We walked through all the buildings and classrooms. I met the athletic director and instantly found someone I got along with. I sat in on a class about the study of Revelations and fell in love with the way they studied the Bible. I visited the basketball gym I had won a tournament in the previous year. Compared to a high school gym, it was huge. I talked about cost with some of the academic counselors and my parents about what financial aid they offered. We found out that because both of my parents were alumni, I received a fifty-percent discount. Coupled with some grants I received and scholarships for my good grades, it was affordable for my parents. Since it was a good school and my parents were excited about the cost compared to other schools, I decided to pick Washington Baptist College as my first choice to attend in the fall.

DESCENT FROM GRACE

"WELL, YOU AT LEAST DRESSED up. Most clients I have come in the courtroom with jeans and a polo shirt," my lawyer said as she scanned my clothes.

I fidgeted, uncomfortable with her stare. "I always try to look sharp. First impressions from the judge are everything from what I have read," I explained.

She checked the clock on the wall before motioning me to walk with her to the door. "Do you have the payment ready? You have yet to give me my retainer."

"Well, here's the thing. I have enough money to pay one of those but not the other."

"Okay? Well give me the money and we will do what we can. I told you months ago the cost of this, you had plenty of time to gather both payments." She scowled.

"You're right but having this looming over my work history records makes it hard to get a job that pays anything. I'm sorry, but I am doing the best I can with what has happened." I shifted back and forth, knowing she could walk out—my problems didn't matter to her.

"I am going to represent you, but I am serious about you paying me the rest of my retainer. Times are tough for you, but it can be much worse without help..."

***

Fall came and it was time for me to head off to college. My parents drove me to Washington Baptist and our goodbyes were filled with sadness. I had a roommate that I was excited to meet but it would be a new experience for me. Since I was an only child, I knew this could be interesting.

Across the hall from me lived Dave, a transfer from Gettysburg College who was also there to play basketball. He had a full beard and shaggy dreadlocks, which reminded me of a hippie, but I didn't care because Dave was personable and friendly. Dave was open about not being a Christian, stating that he was there only because his parents made him. I saw the opportunity to be a testimony to Dave and I loved Dave's honesty. We became great friends, often finishing our classes around the same time and then heading down to the gym to work out and play basketball.

During the year, I soon learned how to be a responsible adult. Mom had washed my clothes and made my bed. She took care of my needs. Being on my own at college, I washed my own clothes and made my own bed, along with other simple chores. I was learning diligence.

Once summer arrived, I worked with my parents' ministry again. It was my seventh summer working with Dad and Mom. I was now an Assistant to the Director. I spent days learning what Mom and Dad did in order to serve. Mom spent hours on the computer doing inventory of the books, typing up newsletters, and preparing for ministries. Dad spent his days on the phone, talking and praying with pastors, and traveling from church to church to build support, both financial and spiritual.

I had more of an appreciation for the amount of hours and work my Dad and Mom would put into their ministry. I had seen the amount of stress my college education was putting on my parents due to tuition cost. Since they were both missionaries, my parents needed financial support to keep me in college.

I kept in touch with Dave throughout the summer through phone calls alone. Text messages were still not something everyone had access to. One day while talking to Dave on the phone, he informed me that he had gone to a church service where the invitation was given for anyone wanting to give their life to the Lord. He told me that he had gone forward and accepted the Lord as his Savior. I was overjoyed to hear the great news and could not contain myself.

"Mom, Dad—guess what I just heard from Dave!" I said bursting at the seams.

"What? Why are you happy?" Mom asked with a puzzled look on her face.

"Dave told me that he went to a church service and asked Christ to be his Savior!"

Right then, my mom, dad, and I bowed our heads and thanked God for the victory that Dave had in his life. That was one of hundreds of memories I have where my parents and I would stop everything we were doing to pray, either to give thanks or ask for God's intervention. My family was built strongly around our faith, and that was a foundational block for the rest of my life.

After my freshman year at Washington Baptist College, Derrick moved from Martinsburg to Sterling, Virginia, and he pressured me to move to Sterling with him. I took a year off from college, even though I did much better my second semester academically, but financially it was still a strain on my parents. I needed a job to earn some extra pocket money.

One day while I was visiting Derrick, we went out to eat at T.G.I. Friday's. While there, I asked the server if he suggested working as a waiter since there was a new location being built near my parents' house.

"It's stressful at times," he said, "But if you do your job correctly you would make money hand over fist."

I applied as soon as I got home. I was hired almost immediately and started training the following week. The training was intense and thorough and I was nervous but excited for the new opportunity. I knew it was going to be difficult, but because of my basketball background I loved the challenge. Within a few weeks I was in the top ten of servers at my location. I made anywhere from seventy to one hundred and fifty dollars a night in tips alone.

One day one of my old friends, DJ, stopped in to have dinner. DJ had worked with my parents' ministry many years earlier. DJ was a shorter guy, with a somber demeanor and was more of a quiet, thoughtful individual. He lived on his own in Martinsburg and invited me over to hang out and watch movies. I stopped over one night and became jealous of DJ's independence. I wanted to hang out there more and more. DJ was going through a tough break up and struggling with depression, so it felt nice to be a friend for him through his tough time. We stayed up late watching old horror movies and wrestling videos. I did not watch wrestling anymore and I wasn't a real fan of horror movies either, but I realized that DJ needed a friend, so I wanted to be there for him. DJ was in between jobs, too, so I helped him get a job at the restaurant to get him get out of the apartment during the day and make new friends. I thought that it might help him get his mind off of his broken heart. We hung out almost every day, and I was glad that he could come to hang out with our coworkers after our shifts.

Things changed as they often do, as people get comfortable and a little too familiar with each other. One night at a smaller hangout, DJ and I were offered pot. Both of us had never done it before but I was curious and had heard that it would make you feel mellow and laugh a lot. I decided to take some and when DJ heard this, he also decided to try. In my mind, smoking would help calm DJ down. When I was handed the joint, I did not feel anything at first but then it hit me. Soon my entire body tingled and I felt almost weightless. Everything people said was even funnier than normal. We had VH1 on and every time the pop-up video would show I laughed hysterically. DJ and I left that night thinking that we should do it again. It would be the beginning of an addiction we both would have for years to come. The thing about pot was even though it calmed you down and turned you mellow, it caused me to have a mental fog.

Another night after work, DJ and I waited to check out with the manager on duty. The manager was busy, so he told us to stick around for about fifteen minutes and wait patiently for him to be free. Another coworker asked if we wanted to smoke weed in his vehicle while we waited. DJ and I both did, and after we cashed out with the manager we went home. I went back to my parents' house and while driving home I realized that I looked different when I glanced in the rearview mirror.

"If I'm quiet," I thought, "I can totally play this off." When I arrived home, it was instantly awkward. First, I had trouble thinking of what to say when Mom and Dad asked questions about how my day went and if DJ was doing well. Every answer I gave was short and unintelligent. I tried to ask them how their day was just to get the focus off myself.

I thought I was in the clear, but then Mom asked if I was hungry.

"Why would you ask that, I just came from a restaurant? Of course I'm not hungry," I said.

Well, you're wasting your appetite with all those sweets," she told me.

"What are you talking about?"

Mom pointed at the large pile of Hershey's kiss wrappers that were next to me. I looked down and I realized the entire time I was talking to my parents I was unwrapping chocolates and eating them. I mumbled some excuse and left immediately. I knew that I could never be around my parents while high again. I started lying to my parents more often. I knew that it was wrong, but I loved smoking marijuana more. I began to hate myself for lying to my parents, but I justified it to myself that it was better than having them worry after hearing the truth.

Most nights after that awkward evening with my parents, I hung out at DJ's house smoking weed and watching movies. I slept over often and DJ's couch became a second bed for me. One night, DJ told me that my old friend Rick lived in the same apartment complex as him. We went over to Rick's apartment and hung out. Rick said he was going to the liquor store so he asked us if we would like anything. I was curious about what alcohol tasted like since I had studied the drinks served at Friday's . Rick went to the liquor store and came home with a bottle of vodka with a jug of orange juice. I tried the mixture and to my surprise, I tasted only the orange juice. I quickly finished my first cup and went and made a second. It went down as fast as the first one.

"If you're going to drink, take your time because drinking too much too quickly can cause you to get sick," Rick warned.

I started to feel the buzz of the alcohol. I was becoming drunk but I didn't want that feeling to be over quickly, so I made myself another drink. "I think I'm starting to feel sick—" I was mid-sentence when I felt a rush of liquid vomit coming up my throat. I threw up all over the front of my shirt. Rick told me that I would have to leave his apartment.

DJ was drunk, too, and felt terrible that he had let me get this sick. He took me around his shoulder and together we both stumbled back to his apartment. The next morning I woke up to an incredibly intense headache and a stomach pain I had never felt before. It was a while before I thought of drinking again.

Months passed and DJ and I still smoked marijuana, getting high almost every night. I would take the money I made from work and spend most of it on drugs and snack food. I felt trapped and empty inside. I numbed my guilt by getting high, but even then I still had a small voice telling me to stop.

I found that if I drank only enough to get an initial buzz, I wouldn't throw up and I was uninhibited enough to talk to people at the clubs we visited or with my friends at their apartments. Although I seemed great to my friends, I felt dead inside. I hated being dishonest with Mom and Dad and I knew they were aware at this point that something was going on with me. I felt that if I continued to live with them, they would eventually find out about my double life.

One night while struggling with deep depression over my faith, I looked to my nightstand where I placed my Bible after Sunday service. I reached out and in a moment of clarity, prayed for God to show me a verse that could help me understand my situation. I opened my Bible and turned to the book of

Romans. My eyes found Romans 5:8, "But God commendeth his love toward us, in that, while we were yet sinners, Christ died for us." I read this verse several times before, but it was like I was reading it for the first time. The word that stuck out to me this time was the word "while." I realized that the farthest I was away from God, He still loved me infinitely enough to send His only Son to die in my place. Ever since I was little, I had struggled with my own salvation. I never shared this with anyone—I taught Bible lessons to children and led many people through the prayer of salvation and yet I questioned my own salvation. I knelt down and began to pray. Going through all this pain of drinking, smoking pot, and partying had caused me to carry an incredible amount of guilt. When I thought of how ashamed I was and that God, the creator of heaven and Earth, loved me in spite of my failures to sacrifice His only son Jesus for me was incredible. This truth was my salvation. I prayed and asked Jesus to come into my heart and be my Savior, something I had done hundreds of times before. But this was different because instead of just saying the "right words," I spoke from my heart.

After that night, I tried hard to live a life pleasing to the Lord. I started attending church faithfully again. I did not have a job other than working with my family in the ministry. Summer was about to end and I had an idea one night while shooting hoops outside to see if I could go back to Washington Baptist College. I sat down with my parents and talked with them about this decision. Although I had made a plan to save up my money for schooling, I had squandered most of my money on partying and drinking. My mom and dad now had the full financial burden of my education.

Fall arrived, I was twenty years old and ready to live the life I was supposed to live. I had a much different plan this time around to make the best of my education. I had file folders and went through every syllabus and marked down due dates for tests, quizzes, and paper assignments. Any reading assignments that had to be transposed into papers I did in advance. I was determined not to blow this second opportunity I had been given.

During the second month of the semester I started training for basketball. The school had just hired a new coaching staff and they were very knowledgeable about basketball. I continued to play and watch basketball through the last two years and felt like my skill level was even better than it was before. With the excitement of basketball season approaching, I received a lot of attention from women. When I talked with the groups of girls around me, I told them about my adventures in clubbing and partying. Some of them thought that the stories sounded fun and exciting. The seed of curiosity was planted, even if it was not my intention.

Washington Baptist College came down on things like going to dance clubs and partying, so I did not want to ruin my second chance. The problem was that the girls wanted to experience the atmosphere. Since I was twenty, I enlisted an older friend, Bronson, from WBC to get a case of vodka for us to drink and then we went to an underage club. We loaded up in the car and drank half of the drinks on the way to the club. When we arrived it just did not have the same feeling. We danced and had a good time, but inwardly I was disgusted with myself. When we left, Bronson asked me what I wanted to do with the rest of the drinks. I instructed him to throw them out, because I was ashamed that I led the group down a dark path.

Basketball season arrived and I was doing well. I scored an average of twelve points and eleven rebounds a game. I had a sneaking suspicion that even though there was no word on the activity of the night we went clubbing, the school would somehow find out. One night the guy across the hall from my room knocked on my door. He was dating the best friend of a girl that I was interested in. He asked me to help him sneak both of the girls into the dorm. I was reluctant, but I agreed to help, letting my hormones take precedence over my values and logic. Sneaking the girls into the room was pretty easy since it was the last room in the hallway, and the entrance was right next to my door. Once the girls arrived, we put a movie on the computer and each of the couples laid separately on the bunk bed. Nothing happened, but the damage of breaking the rules weighed on my mind.

During the next two weeks, my life took another change. First, I got news from home that my parents were barely able to make payments for my education. The money they had was going to medical bills for my mom—she had been experiencing severe heart problems and needed hospital treatment. I didn't know how to deal with this news. I never faced the possibility of Mom's mortality.

Then, a day before the semester ended, I was called into the administrator's office. They told me that the alcohol I paid for and was bought by Bronson was given to the girls that went clubbing with them that night. The girls snuck the alcohol into their dorm room and their roommates found them drunk. The administration told me that they would deliberate and let all parties involved know their decision.

I sat in my room stressed, exhausted, and depressed. Bronson stopped in to say that since he bought the alcohol for minors, he would probably be expelled. I felt I had to do something. I knew that things were not going to get better and if I was expelled, I could go home and help Mom. I also knew that my family would no longer have the financial burden of my tuition. I decided to compose a letter to the school board confessing everything, taking the blame for convincing Bronson to buy the alcohol, talking the girls into drinking, and telling them to take the rest of the alcohol into their dorm. I apologized to the school and asked for help through Christian counseling with alcohol addiction and begged them to let me stay. I wrote that if anyone became expelled it should be me. I printed the letter, put in into a sealed envelope, and placed it under the door of the faculty office. I waited patiently in my room. I packed up all of my things and prepared for the worst-case scenario. I hoped that I would be the only one punished and that the board would find compassion and get me the spiritual help I needed. But unfortunately, I was called into the office the next day and found out that Bronson and I were both going to be expelled. Not only was I expelled, but the school gave me a restraining order from the college. I was no longer allowed to set foot on campus again.

I was heartbroken. I let my family down and was being asked to leave without being given help with my alcohol addiction. The only positive outcome was that Brethren Bible let the girls stay without expulsion. At first, the anger and injustice that I felt was something that I held not only against the WBC, but against the institution of organized religion in general. But then I remembered the humility of Brethren Bible Christian Academy and I knew that it wasn't the entire Christian community. I knew I was at fault and had broken the rules. I desperately needed help but when I reached out to the Christian community, they decided to help by closing doors.

THE FARMHOUSE

EVEN THOUGH I WAS DISAPPOINTED about my expulsion, I was grateful that I was home to help my parents while Mom struggled with her heart issues. When I arrived home, I looked forward to hanging out with my parents and trying to better my life. I mowed the enormous yard, helped with office work, and kept the house clean. I was determined to live a life more pleasing to my family and to the Lord. But as with all my goals to work towards pleasing others, I ended up serving myself instead. As soon as I got back home I hung out with DJ, who lived back home at his dad's house, three houses from my parents. When we hung out, we would either play basketball, get drunk, go clubbing, or smoke marijuana

I acted out with my bad habits again but inwardly I struggled to do the right thing. My grandfather was recovering from a shoulder surgery and needed to go to physical therapy. I loved spending time with Grandpa so I insisted on driving him to physical therapy. Grandpa was in his seventies, but he had worked on the farm all of his life. He was used to hard work, and I respected him a great deal. Grandpa was a quiet man, so I wanted to spend this time with him in order to get to know him more. On those drives, I felt less like a failure and more like I was where God wanted me. Of course, during the evenings I still drank and smoked pot. My desire to drown out my depression outweighed my desire to please the Lord.

One day I got a call from Derrick. He was back in town to visit and wanted to see if I was up for some basketball. When Derrick came over, he brought his younger brother Kevin with him. Kevin used to tag along with

Derrick some days when they were in high school, just in case they needed one more player to make a full game. I remembered Kevin as the quiet little kid that always hung out with us out of boredom. Years had passed since high school and Kevin was now eighteen. He was much taller now and obviously hit the gym every day. Kevin was a good-looking kid and in my opinion, a well-behaved kid. Kevin played basketball almost every day since Derrick and I graduated high school, so his skill level had increased immensely. That night when we were hanging out, Derrick told me that he was worried because Kevin was so shy and had trouble making friends. Derrick asked me to keep an eye out for Kevin and try to include him in hanging out as much as I could. I remembered what Derrick's friendship meant to me, so I wanted to help in any way I could. From that point on, any time I was going somewhere to hang out, play ball, or even spend time with a group of friends, I was sure to include Kevin. Although Kevin was shy around others, he opened up around me. I grew to build a deep friendship with him, looking to Kevin and Derrick as brothers.

That year I turned twenty-one, and I was tired of getting into arguments with my parents about being out late every night. I began looking for a place to live where I wouldn't worry my parents and I could still keep an eye on Mom. DJ and I were willing to live together so that I could have our own space and as roommates our rent would be cheaper, but we needed a good house to find first. Another mutual friend of DJ and me needed a place to live, too. Chris was twenty years old and outgoing. He was a good-looking guy with dark black hair and brown eyes who also enjoyed drinking and partying. Chris also had a church background and lived a life away from the Lord's will. I felt that the three of us would get along great, unfortunately we couldn't find a place close enough for Chris and DJ's commute to work.

One night, Derrick called me and told me that our mutual childhood friend Jeff was coming back from his time in the Army. Jeff had a quiet disposition and spent most of his time on the Army base working out. Now he was very muscular and intimidating to others, yet I always remembered how kind-hearted and compassionate he was.

I greeted Jeff with a big hug and grateful handshake for his service in the military. That night Derrick, Jeff, Kevin, and I went out for drinks. Jeff told Derrick and me that he was moving in with his older brother, Jimmy, in an old farmhouse. He told us that Jimmy had six-bedrooms and that Jeff had mentioned that if they were both to move in they could hang out more often and even throw the occasional party at the house. Derrick was first to agree to move in. I jumped at this opportunity to get away from my parents and the prospect of holding big parties seemed so fun to me.

Once I moved in, I got a job with T.G.I. Friday's this time in Frederick, Maryland. The managers there were the same ones in Hagerstown years before. While at the farmhouse, I helped clean the house, cook food, and straighten up. The house was huge to say the least. It had a huge concrete wrap-around porch with two staircases. The downstairs had an office, study with a bathroom, a large open living room with dark, rich wooden floors, a large wrap-around couch, and an expensive music system and speakers throughout the entire house. There was a large kitchen with an island and enough room for a dining room table and even another couch. Behind the kitchen was a large walk-in pantry with lots of space for storage. The upstairs had four bedrooms and a full bathroom, with a staircase that led to two other large rooms. The outside yard was large and was surrounded by fields and barns. This would be the setting for some of the craziest parties that Derrick, Jeff, Jimmy, and I would ever see.

Halloween came that year and this was my chance to make a name for myself at work. Derrick and I constructed a flyer for a Halloween party that would be the unveiling of the magnificent house and the setting for many parties to come. I asked to post the flyer and my managers told me that if I threw a party where all the staff was invited, my employment would be held responsible if my coworkers did not show up the following day. I agreed.

That night I got off work early and heard from all the staff members that they would be there. I rushed home and to my surprise, Jimmy and Jeff were so excited that they had already prepared the entire house. The empty living room was filled with black lights and the wrap-around couch had white sheets thrown over it so the couch would glow in the dark. There were couches on the porch for people to go and smoke. Jimmy spent over a thousand dollars in mixed alcohol. The kitchen was setup as a place for me to be the bartender and make drinks for the guests. Since Jeff and Jimmy didn't really know a lot of people, they relied on my coworkers to be our main guests. Ten p.m. came and only a handful of people were there so everyone thought the party was a bust. My roommates and I sat on the porch, watching the road from afar, anticipating that all the lights we saw passing down the road were people coming to our party.

Around midnight a stream of phone calls came on my cell phone. Everyone had worked late and took time to get ready. They were all headed there now. Troves of vehicles headed down our long driveway while Jimmy stood outside directing traffic. Almost a hundred people were there and the party was hopping. Everyone was amazed at the size of the house and the bass music thumped throughout the rooms. The dance floor was full of guys and girls laughing and dancing, the porch was packed with people talking and smoking, and the kitchen was full of people drinking and taking shots. Jimmy, Jeff, and I were thrilled at the success of the party. We knew even though this was a big turnout, the word would get out fast about this house and all of its possibilities.

Morning came, and I still hadn't gone to sleep yet. In order to not upset my roommates, I started cleaning the entire house. There were people in every room passed out, and every couch had at least two people on it. I remembered what my managers said to me, so I went around the house and woke everyone up asking if they worked that day. I was able to get everyone to work on time, although most were still hungover from the night before. I had to work that night and when I arrived I was greeted by some very hungover coworkers. They laughed about some of the memories from the night before and asked me when the next party was. I knew my roommates loved the attention they received from the party and had made a ton of new friends. I told my coworkers they could come over that night to hang out and chill. Word quickly got out that there was going to be another party and people started asking me if they could invite their friends as well. I called Jimmy and Jeff and told them what was happening. They were excited and told me to bring them over. For the next three nights, there were back-to-back parties. The house still had plenty of alcohol, but people chipped in here and there with snacks and money.

And so for the next four months, five times a week there was a party going on at the farmhouse. It became the center social hangout spot for all the twenty-somethings in Frederick and the surrounding areas. Everyone wanted to be a part of it. The number of party guests would fluctuate from 100-200 people each party. Jimmy, Jeff, and I became well known in the area for throwing the best parties. With every party that happened and with the constant drinking of alcohol, drama followed. Bands that were starting to make it big from the Baltimore area would show up and bring their groupies to hang out with us as a thank you for inviting them to the party. They even asked me to set up and play a set some nights. All relationships formed in the restaurant started at the farmhouse during party nights, and all breakups were usually a result of drama happening at the farmhouse as well.

One night during a particularly rowdy party, I was in the middle of the dance floor drinking and moshing with some of the other guys. One overzealous partygoer swung his head forward, and when he thrust back he slammed his head into the tip of my nose. I felt intense pain as my nose streamed blood like a strong faucet. I screamed in pain and ran to the kitchen sink. I stood at the sink and thought that my nose had been driven into my head. I thought I was going to die, so I prayed from my soul. My nose stopped bleeding immediately, and I had this overwhelming calming feeling that I was going to live. Since I was intoxicated, I did not think much more about it. I cleaned myself off and went to bed. The next day I went to see my parents and Mom asked me a question out of the blue.

"What were you doing last night at two a.m.?"

I immediately thought back to the party and my nose.

"Why would you ask such a question?"

"God woke me up," she told me, "and He told me that you were going to die that night. So I prayed for God to spare your life and take mine instead."

I never told Mom what happened, but that moment never left me. I knew that God spared me that night because of Mom's prayer.

It seemed as though I was a king around town. Everywhere I went people came up to me to be my friend so that I would invite them to my parties. But when I was alone, I felt dead inside. When the parties first began, I was thrilled—these parties made me feel alive. But as time wore on, the drinking every night became old and the attention I received from people was a front for them to get what they wanted from me. I would call Mom on quiet nights and just hearing the worry in her voice broke my heart. She told me about her deteriorating health and how she prayed for me every night and longed for me to come back home. The emptiness that I thought I could fill with popularity was now an even bigger hole. During the nights I went to my room and grabbed my Bible to read and I longed for a close relationship with the Lord again.

I went to Derrick's room one night and had a heart-to-heart discussion about the parties. I told him that I felt trapped once again and that I missed being near my mom. Derrick told me that the best thing to do would be to move back home so I could be close to my mom and get away from the craziness of the farmhouse. I agreed and was thankful for the good advice—I always respected Derrick because of his candor and honesty.

Once I decided to move, I immediately told Jimmy and Jeff. At this point, there were so many people begging to move in with Jimmy, he did not mind that I wanted to move out. The parties at the farmhouse were bigger than Jimmy or Jeff or me. I warned Jimmy to be careful because one day soon the police would come and it would be bad news for everyone there. And just as I predicted, a few months later an epic blowout party was held at the farmhouse with over 500 people attending. The field next to the farmhouse was filled with cars and trucks. The basement that was once empty was now the spot where four kegs were held on ice and two beer pong tables held tournaments. Outside was a massive bonfire, and near it was a giant trampoline drunk people enjoyed. I showed up with Kevin, DJ, Chris, and a few other friends. Within an hour I saw that the farmhouse that was once an empty house with one lonely person living there became a spot for not just drinking, but drug use, debauchery, and fighting. It had become too big and uncontrollable. I gathered my friends and we left the house. We received word later that night that the police showed up and several of the people that were there, including Jimmy and Jeff, faced multiple charges. I was thankful I left when I did. No parties were held at the farmhouse ever again.

WHEN TRAGEDY STRIKES

I MADE THE DECISION TO move in with DJ and Chris. We were going to rent a house a few houses from my parent's home, so I could keep a watchful eye on my mom. Kevin still came over to hang out, although Kevin's parents pleaded with me to stop letting him come over. They even went to my parents and all four met together with me to plead with me to live a better life. I felt so judged and angry with them that I hardened my heart to their pleas. In my mind, I made a promise to Derrick years earlier to take Kevin under my wing, and I was not going to back out of a promise.

I started working out again at a local gym and during my time there, I became friends with one of the associates that worked at the front counter and was also a trainer. Jackson was a former college wrestler and football player who carried himself with a proud, arrogant demeanor. He had brown hair that was always gelled, and I considered him to be a "pretty boy." One night, Jackson asked me if I wanted to go out for drinks at a bar near the college Jackson was attending. Jackson struggled with his anger when he would drink, and it caused me to have sympathy for Jackson since I also struggled with my anger and would often lash out in fits of rage when I got angry.

I invited Jackson over to my house to meet DJ and Chris. Jackson became someone who would hang out with us often, coming over to the house to drink, smoke, and watch movies. My parents still lived a few houses down, so when we would get wasted, Jackson and I would walk over to my parents' house and get into their stock of candy and peanut butter cups they collected for their ministry. We gathered some of the candy and took it back to my house for all the guys to share. I knew it was stealing, but I lived my life in a constant mental fog.

Mom's health continued to decline. Every time I visited, we were at each other's throats. I lied to her constantly and tried to keep the truth from her so she would not worry. She was now at fifteen percent lung capacity and could not walk across the living room without being out of breath. One day, Dad was on the phone with local pastors raising finances for ministries and without thinking of her situation, asked Mom to get him something in the other room and bring it to him. When I heard my dad, I lost all control and lashed out at him and even tried to fight him. Despite her weakened state, Mom got in the middle of us and quickly broke up the confrontation.

Mom was told that she had to have open heart surgery in order to repair the holes in her heart and replace two of the valves with pig valves. I was intensely worried—for weeks I woke up in the middle of the night and cried at the thought of losing her. I visited my parents often and prayed with Mom. She worried so much for me and she told me I was in God's hands. She warned me of my wickedness and told me I needed to come back to the Lord. I loved Mom so much— she was the only one that I would allow to say these things to me.

Surgery day arrived and Mom had her operation at John Hopkins Medical Center in Baltimore, Maryland. I prepared myself for the worst—I didn't want to be surprised by anything. Thankfully, the surgery went well and I visited Mom with Grandma and Aunt Mary. Mom's medication was strong and it caused her to be extremely giddy. She was thrilled to see me and kept repeating to me how nice my new shoes were. She told me that she worried about my anger and wanted me to get the right help to deal with it in a proper way.

A few weeks later Mom was set to come home. I thought that all the stress and preparation I had put myself through about Mom had ended. That night I went to my parents' house and had dinner with my grandparents, Aunt Mary, and Mom and Dad.

As we grabbed hands and prayed, Mom yelled out Dad's name and immediately slouched in her chair unconscious. Grandma went to call 911 but could not find the phone. In a panicked rage, I swore at Grandma and I was immediately ashamed. I jumped to my feet and rushed out the door. There was a fire hall up the street from our house and I ran down the street toward it. I pounded on the door so hard that I cracked the glass on the gate of the fire hall's garage. I saw my Grandpa at my parents' house outside looking on. The fire hall was empty so I rushed back to the house. On my way back, one of our neighbors who was a part-time paramedic heard the call on his radio and pulled into the driveway. As I walked up the driveway Grandma came outside of the house. I started weeping and crying while Grandma held me tightly. I apologized for yelling at her and she instantly forgave me. We held each other weeping on each other's shoulders. Luckily, the ambulance pulled into the driveway quickly. The neighbor who had rushed over performed CPR on Mom and resuscitated her back to life. She was rushed to the hospital and the doctors were able to airlift her back to John Hopkins. Mom was going to be okay. She had been given several different kinds of medication and she had an allergic reaction to one of them. She stayed in the hospital for a few days and then went back home.

Aunt Mary and Grandma came and helped Mom with bathing and cooking during her recovery process. They prepared a daybed on the enclosed finished porch for her so she would not have to walk up the stairs to go to bed. There was a full bathroom next to the porch as well, so all her needs were localized.

I tried to get my life back on track, knowing that I had not even been to church in several years at this point. I promised Mom I was going to go to church with her the next Sunday. That Saturday evening, Derrick came back into town and several of my friends went to a local house party. I thought that it would be okay to go for a few hours, make an appearance, and then leave to go home. I had full intentions of going to church the next day. Everyone drank heavily but I was determined to have only a few and leave. I started drinking, as I did so many times before, and I quickly became intoxicated.

"Just a few more drinks then I'll call it a night," I thought.

I always hated the taste of alcohol so I would chug the drinks fast to finish them before I had the taste of it in my mouth. The more I drank, the more I became loud and obnoxious.

Through loud joking and mocking of some of the guests, I got into a fight with one of the visitors. I hit the guy and picked him up above his head and slammed him into the ground on the front lawn. When Derrick saw the rage that I had and the fool I had made of myself to everyone else, he pushed me and told me to stop. I pushed Derrick back and told him that I had to leave anyway. I got into my car and Derrick immediately grabbed me. He tried to take away my keys but as we argued, I felt sick with the same feeling I had the first time I drank.

I leaned over and started to vomit. I seemed to have an endless amount of liquid in my system. When there was nothing left, I dry-heaved. Even sitting down in my car caused me to feel dizzy. I drank water when my friends suggested it, but anytime I drank anything I threw up again. Even in all the confusion, I could not get the thought of disappointing my mom and breaking my promise to her out of my head. Finally, while sweating and feeling disgusted with myself, I passed out in the driver's seat of my car.

The next morning, I woke up to Derrick checking in on me. I got my keys and left sober, but hungover. I went straight home and passed out in my bed. Later that evening, after I had recovered, I cleaned myself up and went over to my parents' house to apologize yet again for lying to Mom.

She sadly looked at me and said, "I love you with all my heart son, but at this point I can't trust a word you say anymore."

I saw the disappointment in her eyes. I felt the pain in her heart. Those simple words tore me up inside. She told me that she prayed for me continually and I knew this was true.

A few months passed and Jackson's birthday was around the corner. I wanted to take Jackson out the night before to celebrate. Before leaving, I went over to Mom and Dad's to check on Mom. She was laying on her bed. Dad had spent the day preparing for ministry and was asleep upstairs. I knelt down at Mom's daybed and gave her a hug. I brushed her hair away and gently kissed her forehead. We prayed together and told each other how much we loved one another. As I left, I looked at Mom laying on her back in her daybed and saw a dim light shining through the window from a lamp post outside. I stopped and surveyed this picturesque moment. I suddenly had a morbid thought. Seeing my mom in the lamplight reminded me of someone in the movies laying there dead in a coffin with the spotlight directed at her face. I told Mom I loved her and left to go out with my friends.

I picked Jackson up and we headed to the bar. I could not get that morbid thought out of my head and I could not figure out why. At the bar I did not drink this time since I was the designated driver. The night wore on and finally around 3 a.m. we headed home. I collapsed into my bed and passed out.

The next morning I woke to Chris yelling at me to wake up. I jerked out of a deep sleep and asked what was wrong.

"Dude, I don't know, but there's a message on the answering machine from your dad and you need to call him now!" Chris had a panic in his voice.

I jolted to my feet and ran to the phone. I called Dad and immediately noticed a sadness in his voice. He told me that when he came downstairs, Mom was slumped over in her recliner like she did a few months before.

"I think she's dead, but I just don't know," he said.

"God wouldn't do this to us after all we've been through," I exclaimed.

After instructing Dad to call for an ambulance and hanging up, I gathered myself and sped down to my parents' house. Dad and I got into a vehicle and drove together to the hospital, following Mom's ambulance. We prayed the entire way.

When we arrived at the hospital, we told the receptionist that we were there to see Mom. The receptionist looked up the room and said he would get the doctor for us. We went over to the doors that led to all the emergency rooms. We waited there for what seemed like an eternity.

Suddenly the doors slowly opened and there stood a nurse and the doctor. They stood there with a somber look on their faces and just shook their heads. I did not have to hear a single word and my entire body grew numb. Dad tried to hold himself together but the sadness was almost too much for both of them. We were led into the room where Mom lay cold and lifeless. A single sheet lay over her with only her head uncovered. We were directed to sit and say our goodbyes. I sat there silent for what seemed like hours. Questions circled in my head of why this was allowed to happen to such a godly woman. Several pastors from local churches heard what happened and stopped in the room to help console my dad and me. I was in such pain that I just sat there numb.

The next several days were filled with planning the funeral services and burial plot. My friends all stopped by my house and surrounded me with their love for my mom and me. Memories were shared and emotions ran high. During the final approval of Mom's appearance before the funeral, I finally wept. Up to this point, I was so numb I couldn't process my emotions. I hugged Dad in a tight embrace. I couldn't believe Mom was gone. My best friend was no longer there.

During Mom's memorial service, I was still in a state of shock. I was supposed to sit in the front row. My home church was one of the largest in the city of Martinsburg and the parking lot was packed. When I arrived with Dad we were greeted with hugs from the ushers and Mom's side of the family. All of us were led to the front row and when I entered the church I could instantly feel every eye on me. I felt the judgment from the glaring eyes. I thought back to the bad decisions I had made and how Mom loved me unconditionally through my shortcomings. I was not going to show these people the benefit of any outward emotion.

The service was beautiful. It was filled with songs that Mom loved to sing. I remembered sitting next to her in church services through the years hearing her joyfully sing these hymns. The speaker's remarks encouraged me and filled my heart with gladness and pride of Mom's testimony.

When the service was over, we walked down the stairs of the church and were met by groups of people waiting to see the family. I hung back for a couple of minutes in order to hold back my tears. When I walked into the room I saw Jeff, Derrick, Kevin, DJ, Jackson, Chris, and Marcus. I asked them to create a wall in front of me to block out the people that tried to talk to me. I didn't have anything to say to anyone that was there—my heart was crushed. The guys formed a barricade and kept people away from me.

That night, Derrick and I stayed up all night talking and laughing about memories of Mom. We spoke of her contagious laugh, her stern talks with me even when Derrick was there, the way she fought for me even when I was in the wrong, our many conversations, the fact that she went to every basketball game I played in high school. She was my best friend, and her love for me would never be forgotten.

THE BIRTH OF A MANAGER

THE COURTROOM DOORS OPENED, AND I felt weak in my knees. My heart was beating out of my chest. The black suit jacket I was wearing covered a white shirt drenched in sweat. I wanted to walk into the courtroom but I could not move—panic set in. My lawyer gripped my arm and motioned for me to enter. An armed security officer stood at either side of the entrance with his hands interlocked in front of him. I felt his stare as I passed through the doors. The grandfather clock outside of the courtroom ticked loudly as my judgement awaited.

***

Some time passed after Mom's passing and I decided it was best for both Dad and me if I moved back home. Mom had been the secretary of Dad's children's ministry and I knew how to do most of her job from helping through the years. Dad was in pain and was extremely lonely. I wanted to be there for him, to take his mind off losing his wife, and to help with the ministry and the house.

Within two months of losing Mom, Dad started to date. I had heard about the problems that kids created when their parents started to date other people and they weren't happy about it, so I did not want to hold Dad back from being happy. The problem occurred when I realized Dad was not just dating one woman. Many times Dad was too busy to hang out with me because he was going on another date with someone different. His behavior was something I was not ready for since Dad was still a missionary—I knew that he wasn't coping well with Mom's passing.

It was a sunny Tuesday afternoon and I had just gotten off work. I was about to drive to the gym to work out when I received a call from Dad. He wanted to meet up for dinner and a movie. I agreed and we went to Buffalo Wild Wings a small sports-themed restaurant that had just opened near the theater. I had heard good things about this place and wanted to try their famous wings. While there, I saw a trainer from T.G.I. Friday's I had worked with years before. Kellie had always been a stern trainer but was also a short attractive girl with sandy blonde hair whom most guys tried to date. Even though most guys were enamored by her, I had thought of her as a friend. Kellie was a manager now and she talked about how great this location was. I knew that DJ was without a job at the time so I asked Kellie if she was hiring.

"Yes, we are! Do you want to come work for me?" Kellie asked.

"Actually, I'm asking for DJ," I said.

"That's okay! You should apply, too. We need some good people on staff." Kellie smiled.

I really hated my current job and didn't have health insurance. Kellie told me that within three months of my hire, she could get me into management with full insurance. I went home and walked over to DJ's house. I told DJ about the opportunity and that Kellie would be our manager. DJ was excited to work with her again and thought it was a good decision.

The first day of my new job started and I sat down with Bill, the director of operations. Bill was professional, articulate, and well dressed. His shirts were starched and pressed, and his hair was trim and proper. Bill was a "no-nonsense manager." Bill told me that the company was all about the development of its employees. He said that within three months, if I worked hard and did what I needed to do, I would be a manager with full benefits. Every time Bill talked I held onto every word. I recognized that Bill was a good family man who had an incredible work ethic and eye for detail. I knew that if I worked hard, being a manager for this company was only the beginning. The sky was the limit with this job. I had to have the same laser focus at this job as Bill.

During my spare time, the guys and I really got into filmmaking—a talent that I would pick up on years later. One night, while sitting around the living room and watching movies, we talked about how to make our own movies. We all had interests in movies, so once I saved up enough money, I bought a video camera and computer with video software. I started writing and directing small home movies as practice with the guys when we would hang out at night. Since DJ was a wrestling and horror movie fan, movies he was involved in had to do with those themes. We rehearsed our scenes and then I shot the footage. Once all the footage was filmed, I sat at my computer and edited the films to come up with a final cut. We sat in the living room and watched the films together. It was great practice in editing and filmmaking.

I had now worked at the restaurant for three months. I was the top server there and even spent most of my days training new servers. I was even given the opportunity to help train new team members at a second location opening soon in Westminster, Maryland.

This was the first time I was involved in a new restaurant opening, and I got to travel and stay in a hotel room for several weeks. Opening day for the new restaurant came and I was nervous. The excitement turned into fear of failure. I felt the pressure of a new store opening. The first shift was extremely busy and the restaurant was on a wait for almost the entire day. But I realized that I was in my element and I was able to make lots of money. The first week was busy and the owner of the franchise even came all the way from Chicago to see the opening.

After a successful first day, I went into work the next morning and was pulled into the office. Bill was there that day and asked me if I was willing to work the next few weeks as a shift leader. This meant that I dressed in a button-down shirt, pressed slacks, and helped assist servers during shifts. I jumped at the opportunity since I knew all I needed was a chance to show Bill and the owner what I was capable of doing.

That night I went to a department store and bought a new button-down shirt. I went to the hotel and ironed my shirt and slacks. I came into work the next day dressed for success and was handed a manager card. To me, this was the key to the kingdom. I could now discount meals, computerize menu items, and had the power to show the higher-ups what I had.

The first night of shift leading was a success. At first, I was nervous to talk to tables of angry guests, but soon I realized the guests appreciated my honesty and communication. I jumped from table to table and helped out as many guests as I could. I realized that guests were less upset if they had previously been visited by me before they had any issues. The more interactive they saw me, the less upset they were if they had any issues.

That night the owner also talked to me and told me he was interested in flying me to Chicago to do complete management training. This was the chance I had been waiting for: I was going to be a manager. I wished in this moment that Mom was still alive so I could tell her the good news.

The time came for me to go back home to my grandparents' house. I got four days off before I flew out to Chicago for my six-week management training. The time spent at home involved celebrating with my family and partying with the guys. It was a sweet time with everyone—they all wished me the best with my new position.

Those four days were short, but I packed my bags and headed to Chicago. My mind was completely focused on learning as much as I could so that I could bring more success to my franchises. The plane ride made me feel like a really important person. I arrived at O'Hare International Airport and I was greeted by the owner of the company, Geoff Stockton. He was a kind-hearted older man, dressed in expensive professional clothing. He had a humble and charitable demeanor. He drove me to the hotel and then took me to the restaurant where I was training. I was told that I knew how to handle myself extremely well in the front of the restaurant, but that I needed to learn how to work in the heart of the house—the kitchen. I spent the next month working in the kitchen, learning as much as I could learn. I often came back to my hotel room and took notes of what I had learned that day.

The wind in Chicago was so intense that it often woke me up in the middle of the night. I began to miss home so much. I called my friends every night and they told me how the friend group was doing while I was gone. Thankfully, I finished up my training a week early and flew back home.

While living at Dad's, I helped when needed and typed up newsletters, business minutes, and other forms for Dad's ministry. I started seeing my home church pastor for counseling sessions. I wanted to live a wholesome life professionally and personally. When I didn't work on Sunday morning I attended church. I started reading my Bible again and tried to write down my thoughts. I still struggled with binge drinking and sometimes I still gave in to smoking pot with my friends, but afterwards I was consumed with regret and disappointment in myself.

Professionally, things were going great for me. I worked fifty hours or more a week and I was even nicknamed by the management team as the "Golden Boy." Everything I attempted seemed to be gold. When I was in the kitchen, I used my gifts of problem solving and communication to rally the kitchen to crush the sales records. When I was on the dining room floor, I walked around like a politician at a convention and shook hands and laughed with the guests. Many nights it seemed there were groups of people that came in just to spend time with me.

On the other hand, Dad was not doing well. Child Evangelism Fellowship found out about his habits with serial dating. I also had a feeling that C.E.F was bearing down on Dad for letting me live there. The committee members on my dad's board still had strong opinions about my personal life. Dad struggled to slow his own negative patterns down, although he was asked to do so by all of our family. It finally came to a head and Dad was asked to resign from the organization. What was even worse was that the house that I had grown up in was owned by C.E.F. Dad and I were both asked to leave immediately.

Dad moved in with his parents. My grandfather was now fighting cancer and both of my grandparents needed help around the house with tasks they could no longer do. I threw myself into my job to distract myself from the burdens my dad and I faced. I often worked over sixty hours. Since I ran on fumes most of the day and I needed to be at my best during work, I started supplementing my lack of energy by refueling with energy drinks. When I was younger and a gym rat, I took workout enhancement pills to increase my energy and workout drive. Now I depended on two to three cans of energy drinks a day to boost my energy and focus to a level that helped me be my best at work. I heard this was not good for me long term, but I was so focused at being successful at work I did not care.

I was doing an amazing job at work so I was promoted from the server manager to the bar manager. The previous general manager was let go and a new more energetic boss replaced him. Parker had a magnetic personality and quickly built a strong relationship with me. Parker was quite intelligent and took me under his wings.

During the end of a shift one day, Parker invited me to go golfing with him the next day. I had never golfed before but I knew that the way to get in good with your boss was to spend quality time with him. I went golfing with Parker and borrowed an old set of clubs from him.

"I must be terrible at golf because I feel so uncomfortable," I said to Parker.

Parker laughed and said, "Well, Daniel, you're using right-handed golf clubs and you're left-handed!"

I loved the scenery of the golf course and enjoyed my time with Parker. My drive and determination to learn golf was strong, so I went out and bought a set of left-handed clubs. I visited driving ranges any chance I got and practiced often. I studied how to hit the ball and used techniques Parker taught me to better my game. I golfed once a week with Parker, something I looked forward to very much.

During those golf conversations, Parker imparted wisdom about life and management to me. I enjoyed the stories Parker shared with me. I thought of

Parker and Bill as two strong male mentors in my life. I found out that Parker was an atheist and even though that was completely opposite to my own personal beliefs, I still respected and learned from him.

Parker sat down with me at work once a week and educated me on how to be a better bar manager. He encouraged me to think of myself as the general manager of the bar. He told me to mimic his own management style to the bartenders. So, I sat down once a week with the bartenders and talked with them about where they were currently at and where they needed to be skill-wise. I helped the bartenders become more efficient in saving and lowering bar costs without resorting to stealing from the company or shorting guests in their drinks.

Soon, a third location was slated to open and I was given the option to move to the Baltimore area to be part of the new management team. I saw it as a huge opportunity, but I knew I had not been very good with my own finances. I told Bill that I was willing to move and open the restaurant, but deep down I knew that was a bad decision.

I spent most of my money on car payments, insurance, rent, and then the leftover was what I used to live paycheck to paycheck. I spent two nights a week out at the local bar near my grandparents' house. I drank heavily during those nights and justified it as a way to learn the wrong and right things the other bars would do. Any time a new drink was served, I asked the bartender for the recipe so that I could take it back to my bartenders.

Church attendance fell by the wayside. I was again being pulled into drinking and the late night lifestyle. I took on this new identity of being a respected boss, but my personal life was in pieces. I sat down with my finances and the reality of me not being able to afford the expenses of a move to the big city became clear. I sat down with Bill and Parker and had a tough conversation about my money issues. I admitted I was going out to the bars and blew a lot of money on drinking. I also admitted that I was not ready to make such a big move yet. Bill tried to let me know that I was missing out on a big opportunity, but I still declined the offer.

The new restaurant was about to open and I assumed Parker would move into a new role. Parker was being groomed to take over a new position as the area manager for all three locations. The overall plan was to open fifteen locations in Maryland over the next five years. Since Parker was now the area manager, my friend and coworker, Kellie, was now the general manager of my location. I was excited for Kellie, and I was happy that she was being given this opportunity.

THE PROMOTION

ONE DAY I CAME INTO work as usual, and Kellie came up to me and asked me to sit down. She told me that her personal life was becoming tough, and that she had just broken up with her live-in boyfriend and that she needed to move out as soon as possible. She asked me to think about the opportunity of moving in with her as her roommate in an apartment. She knew my living situation was about to be in jeopardy, so she saw it as a chance for both of us to help each other out. I agreed that becoming roommates was a good answer to my issues, so we decided to move in together.

It was pleasant living with Kellie. We got along very well together and never fought. We were both obsessive about cleanliness so that made it nice. Kellie had a new boyfriend who visited once in a while, and he was quiet but friendly. The living situation wasn't something that my parents would have approved of, but since it was only as friends and nothing else, I did not feel it was wrong. We respected each other's space and spent most of our days working opposite schedules. Kellie, being the general manager, worked mainly the day shifts. I preferred working the closing shifts so I would work late nights.

A year passed and I was now twenty-seven years old. I began to save some money and although I was doing better with drinking, I still went out occasionally. I was given another chance by Buffalo Wild Wings to open another restaurant, but this time in College Park near the University of Maryland. Since I was at a more stable time in my life, I thought this was my chance to move up within the company. One night, Kevin, Jeff, and I got together to go out. Jeff told me that he lived in a house he was renting from one of his friends and that his friend was about to move out and was going to rent the house fully to Jeff. The house was located right outside of Frederick. This was a straight commute for me to go to College Park from there. I asked if I could move in with him and after Jeff asked his friend and negotiated the cost of rent, I accepted.

I was excited for the move and I decided to go out one night for drinks. But as I was leaving the bar, I was pulled over by a police officer. I'd had only two drinks so I thought I was going to be safe. I performed a breathalyzer but those two drinks pushed me over the legal limit. I was taken into the police station and charged with a DUI. I knew this was long overdue since I had struggled with alcohol for so long and had driven in much worse conditions many times before.

I got a lawyer and went to court for my DUI. My lawyer was shrewd and knowledgeable. He used the facts that my dad was a missionary and that I had no prior convictions to my advantage. I was sentenced to perform eight weeks of alcohol awareness classes and to pay a court fee.

During the time that I went to my alcohol awareness classes, I also commuted to College Park. During the day I conducted interviews to hire the staff for the new restaurant and in the evenings I went to the classes. This time, it opened my eyes to the damaging effects of alcohol addiction. This was my wake-up call and I was going to make a change in my life. For the next year, I quit drinking and instead focused intently on the new restaurant.

With the new restaurant, I had a new general manager as a boss. Damon was a firm leader but had a playful side if you followed the rules. He liked me for my knowledge and hard work ethic.

Training began and I was more focused than ever before. I knew that if I could use this time to better my management skills and learn as much as I could, a promotion would be right around the corner for me. The new team of employees consisted mostly of college students, all of whom were eager to learn and make money. Many of them paid their own way through college and this helped me realize that people who have a lot to lose worked much harder than people who lived off their parents.

My first day at the new location came and went. The restaurant had built a level of excitement like none of the managers had ever seen previously. For the next eight weeks, that location generated over $100,000 every week. In less than two and a half months the College Park location grossed over a million dollars in sales. This caused the franchise to strike while the iron was hot. They broke ground on another location in Bowie near a shopping center. Damon told me that the company wanted me to be the assistant general manager of that location. I was now one step away from my goal, and all my focus for the past year was finally paying off.

I interviewed and hired staff for Bowie location. Even though the location was only ten minutes away from the College Park location, the staff was much more diverse. They were all friendly and knowledgeable on how to please a guest. I missed the staff I previously worked with, but I was excited about the opportunity to impart knowledge on these young people's lives.

Bowie opened in the summer of 2009. Summertime is not usually a great time for sales in the restaurant. The sales were not nearly as high as College Park had opened to, but they were nonetheless still impressive. The location did a large amount of carry out orders so they were often not busy inside the restaurant. I thought of my position as an assistant principal, the one who enforced the rules to everyone. Since this mindset was different than the management style I had been under for so many years previously, it was emotionally draining to me.

Damon was now appointed as the second area manager for both of the new locations. Damon went from being someone who was mellow and able to laugh to someone who seemed tense and stressed out all the time. Damon constantly challenged me to be stricter and more no-nonsense. My stress levels were at an all-time high. I had to have a clear mind and upbeat persona always. I chain smoked all the way to work and back home and drank energy drinks constantly to keep myself alert.

The day before my twenty-eighth birthday, I closed the restaurant around 3 a.m. and drove to Frederick. I arrived home around 4:30 a.m. knowing that since I had to wake up the next morning at 6 a.m. and go back to work to open up at 8 a.m., I couldn't go to sleep or I would sleep in, so I thought I would lay on my bed and watch some television, then head to work after an hour or so. I started watching a movie and because all the energy drinks had worn off, I could not stay awake any longer. I thought if I took an hour nap I would wake up and go to work afterwards.

I woke up to the sound of my cell phone alarms going off repeatedly. I opened my eyes to the sun hitting me in my face. I realized I had overslept when I looked at my phone. It was past 10 a.m. and the sounds from my phone were the voicemails and calls from Bill and Damon. I immediately panicked and called Damon. I apologized for oversleeping and tried to explain the situation. Damon told me to get to work as soon as I could, but I could hear the underlying anger and disappointment in his voice. I jolted out of bed and threw on the clothes I had laid out just hours earlier. I rushed out the door and chugged several energy drinks on my long drive to Bowie. I dreaded coming into work and being yelled at for being so late.

I walked in the front door of the Bowie location and to my surprise, the store was not busy at all. Bill and Damon were standing near a table and flagged me over. I knew this was going to be an extremely unpleasant conversation. I sat down and expected a verbal assault of insults and angry words. To my surprise, both Bill and Damon looked at me and smiled. They said that this was supposed to be a great day for me even though it definitely had not started out that way. Bill told me that they were about to open another new location in Rockville. Bill told me that all of the hard work they had seen from me had paid off and they wanted me to be the general manager of this new location.

I was beside myself and I didn't know what to say or do. I thanked both of them and told them that once I was able to write my own schedule, I would not set myself up for failure like this again, nor would I do that to my own management team. I went home that night excited for the new promotion and I vowed to make Rockville the most successful location to date. For four years, I had fought through my own personal and professional struggles to get to this point. I thanked God for giving me the strength to make it and the opportunity to better my life. I wished in that moment I could call my mom and tell her what kind of life I had made for myself.

Rockville had a management staff of coworkers I had groomed from when they were team members, so I felt personally responsible for their success. This was a very big personal step for me.

During the next two months, they held hundreds of interviews with potential team members. I personally hand-picked all the ones that had great personalities and hard work ethics. I spent hours each day on the phone with contractors, vendors, local businesses, and staff members.

Damon was a great guy outside of work, but the pressures to be successful turned into lashing out against me and two other general managers in Damon's area. The hours were long and brutal at times, but I was determined to have this opening be the best one yet.

BAD DECISIONS

IN THE MIDDLE OF DOING several tasks at once, I was asked to meet one of the women applying to be a bartender for my location. Her name was Alicia. She was currently working as a bartender and had several years of experience at a well-known restaurant in Rockville. She wanted to pick up a second job during the day and work at the other location at night. Finding bartenders that wanted to work the day shift was hard. I looked over Alicia's application and realized that she had a good bit of experience as a bartender. I came up with a list of questions to ask to see if her needs met that of the restaurant.

After reviewing her application in my office, I let her in for the interview. To my surprise there sat a quiet and composed woman. Alicia was a light-skinned black girl with long jet-black hair and greenish hazel eyes. She was beautiful. She had a timid demeanor and was educated according to her application. Alicia spoke articulately and professionally. She started working at the other restaurant while attending college and the money she made was to help pay off her student debt. She answered every one of my questions with accuracy and intelligence. I asked her if she would be willing to start as a server and move up to bartender later. Alicia said she was willing and that was all I needed to hear.

"Congratulations Alicia, you're hired!" I said joyfully.

I loved being the one to tell people that they were hired since it gave joy to people when they received the good news. I shook Alicia's hand, stood, and went off busily working on several tasks I had put off in order to hold the interview.

I was in charge of introducing myself to all of the local businesses. I loved going from business to business telling people I was the general manager of the new "big" Buffalo Wild Wings. I quickly used my personality to build relationships with many of the other businesses in the area. My location was much smaller than most of the other restaurants, so they ran with less staff members. This would save on labor costs and help bring in more money.

It was a chilly December morning and the anticipation of opening day was upon us. The staff was trained and ready to make some money. The management team was focused and I was locked in mentally. The Rockville location opened at 10 a.m. and business was booming. People were waiting to get in, which made the atmosphere even more exciting. That first evening they had football, basketball, and hockey games playing on the televisions. The place was packed and I felt like a king and this location was my kingdom. I had put so much blood, sweat, and tears into getting to this point, and nothing was going to hinder me from being successful.

The beginning of 2010 came, and with it came one of the harshest winters in history. A few weeks after opening day, the area was due a big winter storm and they were told that the "mother of all snow storms" was coming. I knew that since this location was in the middle of the town, there was no way for my management team to make it in once the storm hit. I also knew that above all of the shops and businesses in the town center were apartments. If it were to snow heavily, there would be a bunch of trapped tenants with nowhere to go. I had an idea.

I told all of my management staff, "Stay home if the snow comes. I will stay the night and close the restaurant." I found seven team members who lived within walking distance of the restaurant and told them that if it snowed, I was going to open the store anyway. They were excited about the opportunity to make money even on a snow day. That night I borrowed a pillow and blanket from one of my coworkers. I slept in a booth in the restaurant and woke up to over a foot and a half of snow on the ground with no end in sight. I opened the restaurant with a small group of five workers: two in the kitchen, two servers, and one bartender. During the daytime it was slow, but I knew there was a hockey game that night, and Rockville had a lot of hockey fans who wanted to watch the game. By six in the evening, the restaurant was packed with guests. The hockey game was on and the crowd enjoyed being out of their apartments. No other location in Rockville dared to be open since there was over five feet of snow outside and snow drifts were as high as ten feet in some spots. The restaurant finished the day with over five thousand dollars in sales, and labor was around eight percent. It was a true success. The next day I told my management team, "Stay home and hopefully the roads will be better the day after tomorrow." I spent another night sleeping in the store and woke up to open the restaurant for plenty of customers. The store made another six thousand dollars in sales.

I slept in the booth for a third straight night, and this time woke to Damon coming into my restaurant. Damon was so pleased with my loyalty to the store he said, "Take the next three days off and get some rest. You've earned it!"

"Thanks, I'm so stiff from sleeping in this booth that my bed in a warm house sounds great!" I replied. I went home thrilled to have come through for the company I loved so much.

Success became something of a regular event for the Rockville location and for my team. During the first quarter, the restaurant was able to turn a profit—something that had never happened previously for any other location.

I had all of this success with my professional life, yet I did not have anyone to share it with once I got home. Jeff was still my roommate, but he started dating a girl and it was getting pretty serious. I wanted that kind of special someone in my life as well.

One day one of my managers came up to me and said, "There is a bartender who has a crush on you, Dan. It's Alicia. She really likes you." I looked up at the bar and almost immediately Alicia linked eyes with me and smiled.

I would never jeopardize my success or career for a relationship with a co-worker, but it did give me another reason to come to work each day. Days that Alicia worked behind the bar were days that I looked forward to very much. She was very pretty and out of my league, at least in my mind. Throughout my day around the restaurant, I would go behind the bar and flirt with Alicia, and she would flirt back. All she had to do to get what she wanted was bat her greenish hazel eyes at me.

"What's happening to me? I'm putty in this girl's hands!" I thought. One day while in a meeting, I received a text message from an unknown number. The text read: "Would you be okay if I quit?"

"Who is this?" I replied.

"Alicia, sorry I got your number from another team member. Hope that's all right." I was very curious.

"Oh hey, what's up? If you want to quit that is your decision," I replied in a calm and cool fashion.

"If I quit can we hang out?" Alicia responded.

I quickly responded, "I will put it to you this way. If you quit today, I'm probably going to ask you out tomorrow . . . Yes we can definitely hang out!"

"I guess there's my answer, I quit!" Alicia answered. I asked her to dinner the following evening and she accepted.

None of the team members knew that Alicia quit. She walked into the restaurant dressed up looking clean, well dressed, and beautiful. Her eyes seemed to glow in the low-lit lights of the restaurant. All the servers working that night looked at her with a pleasant surprise. I came around the corner and was dressed up in a different outfit than my uniform. Everyone working that night was puzzled. I told them that she quit the day before and that I asked her out. The team stood in shock watching us leave together.

Alicia and I sat at dinner for hours and talked about our lives and told each other about our future goals in life. Alicia told me that she wanted to find someone who would love her in spite of how she looked, even if she was ever in an accident and could no longer walk. That struck a chord with me because deep down I always wanted someone to love me for who I was, someone that would love me unconditionally like Mom did. Alicia told me that she was a simple girl, meaning she didn't need expensive things to be happy. I loved hearing that, since I was terrible with my finances. She checked every box off my list for a potential wife. At this point in my life, I had dated many women, and within an hour into those dates I always found a reason I didn't want a second date.

Alicia was different and she had a good head on her shoulders. I asked Alicia about her faith, which was extremely important to me. She told me that she believed in God but did not go to church. I asked if she considered herself a Christian. She asked me what that was, and I explained. She told me she was not a Christian based on my answer. I should have known at that moment to get away quickly. The Bible says, "Do not be unequally yoked." I thought of this verse, but I had already opened myself up to starting something more with Alicia. The date ended when I walked Alicia back to her car and we exchanged a hug.

The next day I felt energized and rejuvenated. I went across the street from my restaurant and walked into the gym. I asked if they could offer me a discount since I was the general manager of the store across the street. They loved my restaurant and told me I had a free membership.

I started working out that day. I weighed myself in and to my surprise, I was over four hundred pounds. I did not get discouraged, though, since this was my starting point. Every day for the next several months I went to the gym and worked out. I started dieting and eating more vegetables. I worked out for three hours after work, then stopped back at the restaurant afterwards and checked in. I was determined to lose the weight and better my health for my sake and the potential of dating Alicia.

One week passed and I was supposed to have my second date with Alicia. I had been looking forward to it all week. I went to the gym and worked out to help motivate me even further. I checked my phone repeatedly and there was no word from her.

"Is she not interested in me anymore? What did I do wrong?" I thought. "A girl of this caliber has to be in high demand, so if I want her to date me, I have to step my game up."

I knew where she worked so I went in after my shift and sat at her bar. I ordered a drink so that I didn't come across as a creepy stalker. She saw me, came over, and started talking with me. She told me she had gone out with her girlfriends and drank too much the night before. She apologized and told me that she would like to go out with me again, just another time.

Several dates went by and I could not figure her out. We would go out and have a great time, but then I wouldn't hear anything from her until I went to see her at work. I figured I was not the only guy she was dating, so I made my dates too nice to refuse or blow off. I spent hundreds of dollars to buy tickets to a playoff hockey game, bought tickets for the bands that she wanted to see, and I even took her out to all the nicest restaurants. Anything I could think of to buy time with Alicia I did. Some weekends she came to my house to stay, and I took her out to nice restaurants or made her elaborate dinners. I constantly spent money on her, but I didn't care because I felt I loved her and wanted to spoil her. If I didn't have something amazing planned, I didn't even hear from her.

For the next three months I spent all of my attention and energy on Alicia and disconnected from the tasks of running the successful restaurant I had helped build. One day while on a date with Alicia, I asked her if she would like to go on a trip somewhere exotic with me.

A few months back, Derrick had married his girlfriend Tammy and moved to the Cayman Islands. He worked for a prestigious telecommunication company there and tried to convince me to come and visit. I asked Alicia if she had ever been to the Cayman Islands and she said no. She got excited when she heard I was taking her there.

I told Derrick the good news and how special Alicia was to me, and that I was thrilled to have the chance to introduce her to Derrick and Tammy. Derrick told me that we could stay with him and Tammy and that they would even be our tour guides around the island.

I got my passport ordered and went online to buy tickets for the plane ride. The tickets round trip were not cheap. I was quickly running out of money even though I had a good job. I was worried I would not have enough money for the trip and so I decided to do something that I would regret for the rest of my life.

Every Friday, I was tasked with writing a check for five thousand dollars and cashed the check for all twenties. I then took the money to the ATM located within my restaurant and deposited the money. I typed in the amount I had deposited and the computer would subtract the money from each transaction at the ATM. I knew that every week there was always about six or seven hundred dollars of twenties left over from the previous week. I knew that if I borrowed five hundred dollars from the ATM and typed it in as the same amount it was supposed to be, I could use the money for my trip. Then when I returned, I would simply pay the ATM back the difference. "No harm, no foul," I thought.

One week before I was going to take Alicia to the Cayman Islands, I took her out for dinner. We sat at the bar and laughed about how much fun we were going to have on our trip. Everything was going great and I had this elaborate plan to whisk Alicia to a tropical island where we would fall deeply in love with each other. I had not had a vacation in two years so to me, this was a real treat.

When I arrived home that night I never received a text from Alicia. "She must have gotten busy with something else," I thought. I went to work the next day with my head in the clouds, excited for our upcoming trip.

When I arrived at work, two team members asked to sit down and talk to me. They told me that they did not want to meddle in my personal life, but the night before they saw Alicia drunk at the bar, all over another guy, and even left with him at the end of the night. I was confused and saddened at what I had just heard so I texted Alicia and asked her if this information was true. She did not respond. This drove me insane and caused me to text and call her repeatedly. She did not respond to any texts or phone calls. I spent every waking moment thinking about how I messed things up with her, and I blamed myself for her behavior.

The night before we were to leave, after I came home from work with the money for the ATM, she called me. Alicia's voice was timid and she had guilt through every fluctuation of her speech. She told me that I probably didn't want her to go with me. I told her that it wasn't true and that all I wanted was to have her with me. I asked her to pack her clothes and come with me on this trip. We met in Rockville early in the morning and headed to the airport. The entire drive, waiting in the airport, and trip on the plane was filled with silence. I tried to reach out and touch Alicia, but she would only rescind her arm like a turtle going back in its shell.

We arrived in the Cayman Islands and it was gorgeous. The weather was perfect and we were greeted by Derrick and Tammy. Derrick gave a huge hug to me and told me how much he had missed me. I was confident that the situation with Alicia would turn around in paradise.

The first four days in paradise Derrick and Tammy tried to get Alicia to speak, but she sat on the couch almost mute. I reached out to hold her and she pushed me away. I blew through money fast and recklessly. Once Friday hit, I decided that maybe Alicia didn't feel comfortable with Derrick and Tammy. I went and rented a nice hotel room closer to the beach where we could stay.

"Maybe she just wants from privacy, she may not want to discuss our personal lives or problems around my friends." I thought.

Alicia suggested they take Derrick and Tammy out for dinner as a way to thank them for their hospitality. I thought that would be a great idea. We went to a nice sushi restaurant and had dinner and the alcohol started to flow.

I was so frustrated and confused that I decided to get drunk. While out at a dance club near the beach, I took a walk with Derrick. I explained the whole confusing situation to Derrick.

"You need to forget about this girl. Alicia is bad news for your overall health and well-being bro!" Derrick said.

"I think I'm in love with her. She told me she loved me, too," I responded. I was always so stubborn and never thought others knew better than me.

Later, we all went out to a Spanish themed night club. Instead of sitting with Derrick, Tammy, and me, Alicia talked to the disc jockey the entire time. When Alicia and I went back to the hotel room that night, she told me that she needed to see other people. I was heartbroken and told her all I wanted was her. We went to bed but I lay restless throughout the night.

The next morning, Derrick called the hotel room and asked if we wanted to have breakfast. I wanted to, but Alicia told me she wanted to explore the island and shop for souvenirs by herself. I spent the day pining over Alicia to Derrick. Derrick and Tammy cared for me, but they were tired of my tears and self-blaming.

Later that afternoon, Derrick and I went back to the hotel room to see if Alicia was there and found an empty room. She was still out shopping and probably trying to avoid me. I saw her bag in the corner of the room and had an idea. I decided to check her cell phone. I reached into the front pocket and grabbed her phone, turned it on, and found over thirty messages from different guys sending pictures and texts asking when they would meet again. I realized that all the money I had spent, all the time and energy I had wasted, and the attention I had pulled away from my successful restaurant was for nothing.

The next day was a silent trip home. No one said a word. Finally, when we got to my vehicle, Alicia asked me what was wrong. I tried to hold it in, but the texts from all the guys I saw on her phone ran through my mind. I told her that all the time I put into her the last six months was a wasted effort.

I saw the effects drinking alcohol had on Alicia and for the first time, I was able to notice how it hurt others first-hand. I wanted nothing to do with drinking anymore, and I now realized how many people I had hurt with my own drinking. I never mentioned Alicia's phone to her because I knew I didn't have to. She knew what she was doing. I dropped Alicia off at her car and headed home heartbroken and miserable.

When I got home I checked my bank account only to find it completely empty yet again. I didn't even have enough money for gas for the next two weeks. When I drove to work the next day, my car started to shake. I looked down at the temperature gauge and saw it was overheating. I pulled over and turned the car off. I popped the hood to find that the radiator was busted. I used my free AAA tow to get myself to work. While at work that day I noticed that the ATM was out of money. I saw this as an opportunity to help myself out of this hole once again. I cashed another check and stole four hundred dollars. Now I owed nine hundred dollars total and I had to pay it back as soon as I could before I got caught. I used the money to fix my car and put gas in my vehicle. I spent the next two weeks eating at work and used the rest of the four hundred dollars to buy food for myself. The next payday came, and instead of paying back the ATM right away I decided I would take care of it later. I figured my bonus came in three weeks and that would be plenty of money to completely replenish the ATM money and I could save the rest to make sure this never happened again.

Three weeks had almost passed and I was beginning to get my focus back. I spent more time at work and I was still able to work out in the evenings. I found a routine and stuck with it. Bonus day came and I was ready to cash the check and return the money I had borrowed from the ATM.

While working one day, I walked around the restaurant as I normally did. When I turned the corner, though, I found Damon at the ATM machine. I knew that it wasn't time to fill the ATM, so I stopped and asked Damon what he was doing. Damon told me that he was asked by the corporate office to run an audit of all the ATM machines. I immediately worried about what I had done. I knew they would find out about the missing money and I could be in huge trouble. That evening, I went over my options. I sat on a park bench near my house and in the quiet of the evening I prayed for forgiveness. I knew there were only two options: wait and worry until they found out what was happening or come clean now with a confession. The latter meant I would be without any money that next week if I paid them the nine hundred dollars I owed.

I made the toughest phone call of my life and called Damon. I told him everything, and that I would pay them back immediately. I told Damon that was the reason corporate asked for an audit. Damon was disappointed and confused about the situation but told me he was going to call Bill and tell him the whole story. I waited by my cell phone for a few hours.

My phone rang, but this time it was from Bill. I admitted everything to Bill and told him I had the nine hundred dollars to pay back the company. I told Bill I needed the finances to fix my car and that I was too embarrassed to come to Bill or Damon about my financial troubles. I thought that since this was my only blemish out of five faithful years of service, the company would have sympathy on me. After a few months I truly expected all would be forgiven. Bill told me that they needed to talk in person, and to wait until the beginning of the week so that all of them could sit down to discuss the matter.

Monday came and I walked up to the restaurant. I was nervous, saddened, and emotionally drained from having the stress of this conversation on my mind all weekend. I walked in and went to a table where the owner of the franchise sat with Bill and Parker. I sat down across the table from all three, and the owner asked to hear my side of the story. I told him exactly what happened and I apologized for my lack of judgment in the situation. I told them that I had the money with me and I was ready to pay them the amount I owed.

To my surprise and disappointment, I was told that the amount I said I took didn't match the records. There was obviously a bigger problem going on. I later learned that Damon had went into all three of the ATMs, and through the course of several months, had taken tens of thousands of dollars. When I went to Damon to confess my own theft from the ATMs, Damon used it as a way to pin all the missing money on me. I was floored and I didn't know what to say. I wanted to tell them that I had taken money out of only my ATM location in Rockville. I asked how much money the company thought I had taken. When they told me the amount was almost fifteen hundred dollars, I quickly pointed out that was not the case. At that point, they asked me if Damon and I had worked together on this scheme.

"No way, I was doing this alone. I know the way this must look, but I didn't work with or know anything about Damon taking any money. Why do you think I went to him in the first place? Am I going to need a lawyer? This is outrageous," I said.

"It will not come to that point. You're going to be fired, and once the investigation is over we will call you with the amount you owe the company. You can settle up at that point," Bill said.

I hoped the company would not fire me. I knew what I did was stealing, but in my mind I was always just borrowing the money. I had full intentions to replace everything I took.

The realization that I no longer worked for the company I loved so much broke my heart. I saw the disappointment on their faces—these were the people who gave me a chance at real success. Bill and Parker were my true mentors, and I let my own stupidity and foolishness steal from them. I was overcome with pain—I wept at the table and begged them not to fire me. It was a stupid lack of judgement, and my heart filled with shame and regret. I apologized relentlessly to all three of them.

The meeting concluded and I had to walk through the restaurant I had worked so hard to build. The team members all stopped to look at me as I walked through the dining room and out the front door.

SUFFERING

TWO WEEKS WENT BY AND I waited for the end of the investigation. I sat in my basement living room day and night, depressed and frustrated. My actions over the last six months replayed in my mind over and over again. The phone rang one day and it was Bill.

"Finally," I thought, "I can pay back the nine hundred dollars and be done with this dark time in my life."

However, Bill told me that the investigation was complete on their end and that I had to pay back fifteen hundred dollars. He also told me that they turned the case over to the police and they were pressing charges.

Though I made some regretful decisions, I was no idiot. I knew how much I had taken from the restaurant ATM and if I paid out all the money I was accused of stealing, I would be admitting guilt for the full amount. I told Bill that I would pay only the amount I actually took. But Bill only said to expect to hear from the Montgomery County court for the hearing date and that now would be a good time to get a lawyer.

Since I could no longer afford to live with Jeff, all I wanted to do was to run. I wished Mom was still alive to cry on her shoulder. I had to go back home.

One day I called Kevin to see if he wanted to play some basketball and afterwards, Kevin invited me to come over and hang out. While I was there, I asked Kevin if anyone lived in the other room. Kevin told me that he had a roommate, but that he was about to move out. I asked if I could move in and Kevin agreed.

I enjoyed my time with Kevin, even with the upcoming court date looming in the future. Kevin bought a video camera and editing equipment and was looking to start a film series on YouTube. Kevin and I liked the same kind of movies, specifically comedies. Kevin asked me if I was interested in filming another sketch. We ended up filming dozens of short sketches. Our creativity helped me stay focused on other things instead of my court case. At night, Kevin and I went out to the bar for drinks and relaxation. I started drinking again, which was yet another promise broken. "Just add it to the list," I thought.

One night while out with Kevin, I heard someone say that drinks were only a dollar if you played the slot machines. I thought that if I played the smallest denominations, I could save a lot of money. I put in a twenty-dollar bill and started playing. Five drinks later and I was about even with almost my full twenty still in the machine. I got bored so I upped my wager to the max bet. When I spun, I won five hundred dollars. I was pretty drunk at this point, so I didn't need to play the slots anymore.

Kevin took me to another bar with a billiard table. We both played pool together and then went over to the bar. There were two ladies standing by the bar, dressed very nicely, that made eye contact with me. I drunkenly stumbled over to the girls and started flirting heavily. One of the girls started a conversation with another guy, so I started talking to the guy. He seemed nice, but before I knew it, we were in an argument about a movie star. Even though the argument was playful at first, it quickly went south. I was so intoxicated that I pulled out a wad of money and made a bet with the guy that I was right. I threw the five hundred dollars on the table. The girl next to me immediately picked it up and said she would hold onto it for us both. The other guy said, "Dude, I'm not going to bet because you're probably right." I smiled smugly and looked at the girl to ask for my money back.

"I don't have your money, my friend does," she said.

Even though I knew she had the money, I laughed it off as if she was joking with me.

"I know I'm coming off as a real jerk here, but you don't know my situation. I need that money. Where is it?" I asked.

The girl ignored me and walked outside with the other guy to smoke a cigarette. Kevin tried to get me to come home, so we went outside and Kevin walked to the car.

"Go ahead Kev and start the car. I'm gonna go say goodbye to the girl and I'll be right there. Don't worry, I got this," I assured him.

The girl became blatantly rude with me, so I tried invoking fear by threatening them. The girl that sat on the curb suddenly jumped up and got in my face. She cursed me and pushed me. I realized I'd had enough of everyone and lost control. I forcibly pushed the girl to the ground. Immediately the guy stood up and punched me in the face. I threw him to the ground but tripped on my own clunky, drunk feet and fell to the ground. We wrestled around on the ground for a few moments. I tried to get up but felt a sharp pain in my eye. The girl had kicked me in my eye socket with the heel of her shoe. Finally, Kevin drove around and saw all three of us on the ground rolling around in a weird drunken wrestling match. He rolled his window down and yelled at me to get in the car. I went to bed that night feeling sore and ashamed of myself. I had hit rock bottom. What kind of man had I become?

The trial was not for another three months and I came face to face with myself. The person others saw was not the person I knew I was in my heart. My depression grew deeper and darker with every passing day. Many days I didn't even leave my apartment and I often did not leave my own bed. The only escape from it all was when Kevin and I filmed a comedic sketch. It was short-lived and the depression reared its ugly head quickly after.

At night, I took walks in the dark and smoked in hopes of relieving some stress. I was always jovial and positive, but I could not mask my shame anymore. I lied awake at night and prayed for God to end my life. I prayed during this time and yearned for God to show His presence, but I felt alone.

I procured a lawyer from the Rockville area. I had to pay seven-hundred and fifty dollars just for the retainer and then another seven-hundred and fifty right before the trial. I knew that even if I paid for a lawyer, I still had to pay for retribution to the company. I considered it would be easier to pay just the fifteen hundred dollars to Buffalo Wild Wings and save the rest of my money, but I knew that I wasn't guilty of stealing all of what they accused me of. I also knew that if I went to court without representation, I would be eaten alive by the judge. I had to fight it with the help of an attorney.

I wanted to use the money from my tax returns to pay the rest of my attorney fees and restitution. But with a month left before the court date, I was still short on my lawyer fees. I sat in my room shaking and upset. I needed God in my life greatly and for the first time in my life, I did not feel or sense the presence of God. I knew I was still a Christian, but I felt God had left me to rot in a jail cell of my own doing. I looked in my nightstand and found my Bible. I pulled it out and decided that to hear God speak I had to read His Word. I prayed a simple prayer for God to communicate through the Scriptures to me, as He once did many years ago. I opened the Bible and turned to the book of Psalms. In Psalm 46:10, I read a verse that would stay with me for the rest of my life, "Be still and know that I am God." I felt confused.

"What does this verse have to do with my situation? Why does the Bible never tell you exactly how to feel and act? How am I going to get the money I need to pay for rent, restitution, and my attorney?" I thought, worried.

I did my taxes and waited for the return. Every day I hoped that when I checked my bank account that I would see the direct deposit. Finally the day before my court hearing, I checked my bank account and the refund was there! I was thrilled and I wanted to celebrate. I went by myself to a local bar and as I sat at the bar drinking, I heard a familiar sound. I turned around and in the back of the bar was a side room where people played slot machines.

My tax return gave me enough to pay for my lawyer and restitution with a few hundred left over, but I remembered how months before I had won five hundred dollars from playing the slot machines. I went to the ATM and withdrew a hundred dollars, then I went to the slots and put twenty dollars in and played small at first. I remembered that my big win came when I wagered the max bet. So, I played a max bet on every spin. I lost my money very fast and soon I realized I had spent it all. I felt that my luck was turning and wanted to go for big money. I went back to the ATM and withdrew another hundred dollars. I played the slot again and went with the max bet every time. Soon, I had lost another hundred. I got up and went back to the ATM a third time and withdrew the maximum allowance for a single day—three hundred dollars. I went to the bartender and ordered a strong drink, walked back to the room, sat down and thought about my next big win. In less than five spins I hit a big line of two hundred dollars. I was back to even.

I knew I should cash out and cut my ties with gambling, but if I left now, I was only even. I kept hitting the button spin after spin. I had five hundred dollars to start out and so I sat there for over an hour. I lost four spins in a row and then won a small amount on the fifth. I drank and smoked while I played. I finally came down to the last spin. My hands were shaking and I was on the verge of an emotional breakdown. I hit the button, and lost five hundred dollars. I was now behind on what I owed my lawyer.

I knew I could not withdraw any more money from the ATM, so I went to the bartender. I asked if I could get two more drinks and a pack of cigarettes and if I could write a big amount on the tip line and use that was a way to draw cash out. The bartender agreed even though that was not legal. I got the receipt and wrote three hundred forty dollars on the tip line. I told the bartender to keep forty dollars and give me the rest in twenties. The bartender handed me the money and I went back to the slots. I put all the money in at once and thought that if the machine read how much money was placed inside it would have to pay some out. I sat there and shook intensely with every push of the button. Sweat poured down my face. I smoked cigarette after cigarette to help with my nerves. I started to realize that I was losing the money extremely fast without even winning small amounts. Within twenty minutes, I lost everything. I hung my head in shame and had a tightness in my chest when I stood up. I was in a haze when I walked out the front door of the bar.

I got into my car and cried. I lost over nine hundred dollars, counting the bar tab and my big tip to the bartender. I hated myself even more and I felt like I deserved to rot in jail. "No matter how many times God helped me get out of a mess," I thought, "I always managed to make bigger problems." I often felt like I was trying to swim up river against a current. Every time I moved forward a foot, I got caught up by the power of the rapids and got swept further down the river.

I now had only enough money to pay the retribution to my company. To make matters worse, my car sputtered the whole way home. When I got home I turned my car off and then tried to turn it back on again. This time the car would not start. I freaked out and cried even harder—my whole body felt sick. I reached for my cell phone and called Derrick. I asked Derrick if I could get a ride from him that next morning to the courtroom since my car died. Derrick instantly agreed and told me he wanted to spend some time with me before the court appearance.

That next morning, I woke up still sick to my stomach. I hoped that the past two days was just a terrible dream. I took a shower and made sure I looked clean and presentable. I put on the one nice suit I owned, the same suit purchased for my grandfather's funeral. I pressed a clean white shirt with starch to look professional and wore my black leather dress shoes that I polished and shined. I grabbed my cell phone, wallet, and cigarettes. I sprayed myself with my favorite cologne. I went downstairs and waited outside for Derrick to arrive.

All I could do was pray that God would have mercy on me. Pride, selfishness, and lust had caused me to betray all the values I grew up believing. All the core values my parents raised me to have I no longer carried near to me. I abandoned a God who sacrificially gave His only Son to die for me, in spite of all the wrong I had done. I asked God for a message of comfort, but the only response I heard was a still small voice saying, "Be still and know that I am God." I thought back to the night before when I read that verse and instantly knew that even if I had stayed home and missed my court date, I would still have enough money to pay for all the costs.

Derrick arrived and drove me to the Montgomery County Courthouse in Rockville. Derrick was quiet on the drive and I sat in self-reflection. I asked God to forgive me for my prideful, arrogant attitude, my lust of money, power, and women, and my disobedience to God for all the years I lived in rebellion. I asked forgiveness for my unfaithful stewardship of my money, for stealing from the company I loved, and for robbing myself of God's peace and blessings. I prayed for God to help me to finally stop my bad habits. I wanted to quit drinking and smoking—I asked God to make me sick of the party lifestyle. I wanted to have peace in my life once again—I told God of my shame and hatred for myself and asked Him to change my attitude and cleanse my soul.

When Derrick pulled up to the courthouse, I was very early.

"Thank you for the ride, man," I told Derrick as I grabbed my things to leave. "You've always been such a good friend to me." Derrick smiled and drove off. I found an ATM and took out the rest of the money I had in my account. I walked around the block to clear my head. I smoked cigarette after cigarette before walking up the courthouse stairs into the lobby. The elevator took me to my floor and opened to a crowded foyer outside of the courtroom. I was still early, so I found an empty seat and waited for my attorney to appear. An hour passed, and while I waited I prayed and reflected on what I did to get to this point in my life.

Finally my lawyer appeared and she did not ask me about the rest of her fee. She told me that she talked to Bill from the restaurant, and that they agreed to accept a restitution amount of nine hundred dollars. I was only being charged with a misdemeanor and after a year, it would be expunged from my records. This was great news!

The court doors opened and the bailiff came in the foyer and told everyone that was waiting that the judge was ready for them. We entered the courtroom and took a seat near the front of the court. The judge had many cases to hear that morning, so it was quite a while before my case was heard. I heard the door squeak in the back of the room and I turned around and saw Bill coming to hear the case. The judge finally called my name and I went with my lawyer to the front. My lawyer was articulate and thorough. She spoke with humility and compassion for me. The judge asked Bill if he, on behalf of the company, accepted the terms that my lawyer had laid out. He agreed and the judge made his sentence. He told me that I was on parole for one year, during which I would be assigned a parole officer that was responsible for collecting the retribution amount in full. The judge said the case was dismissed and slammed his gavel. I looked back to find Bill so I could thank him, but he had already left. I walked out of the courthouse with my attorney, and she finally asked for the remaining balance of my case. I told her I did not have it but that I did have the balance for retribution. She took the money and told me it would be in escrow until the restaurant received the amount. She warned me that I needed to be diligent in paying her the remaining balance, otherwise she couldn't work on getting my case expunged from my records.

ROAD TO REDEMPTION

I WALKED OUT OF THE courthouse feeling like a new man. I was so relieved that God had helped me through this terrible mistake.

"Thank You, God, for getting me through this," I prayed. "Please provide for me as only You can with a renewed heart."

I never wanted to lie to myself or anyone again. I was going to be the man God wanted me to be. Derrick arrived shortly after I got out of court and rejoiced with me when he heard the news. We hugged each other and I could smile once again with this burden lifted.

I went home that day thrilled for the upcoming opportunities. I checked my email and found a letter from a job hunter. I was excited when I read this, especially that the man wanted to speak to me soon.

The man told me of a management opportunity in Rockville. It was a restaurant with a similar theme as the company he started within Rockville. He set up an interview for me for later that week. I went outside to try to start my vehicle, but it was completely broken down. Now that I had a job interview, I just needed transportation to get there. I talked to my Uncle Eugene, and he had a spare vehicle that he let me borrow.

I went to the interview dressed in my suit. I sat down with the manager and right away we hit it off. I was knowledgeable of the restaurant business and honest with what happened at my last position. The interview ended with a job offer and a firm handshake of acceptance. I had a job and started training in Rockville in a week. Now I needed to figure out my car situation and find a place to live closer to Rockville. I used one of my social media accounts to post the good news and to ask my friends that lived in Rockville if they knew a place to rent. Within two minutes, I received a message from one of my ex-employees offering to take me in as a roommate. God provided a new job and a place to stay for me within a week. I made the commitment to abstain from drinking and partying from this point forward. God was no longer silent in my life—in fact, He was reminding me how good it is to follow Him instead of my own desires. My relationship with God became something more important to me than my partying lifestyle after my court date. I finally found peace in my life.

Moving day came and I still had not found an answer to my car situation. I prayed and was startled by my phone. Uncle Eugene called and offered to sell me his well-maintained sport utility vehicle. I would make monthly payments until the vehicle was paid in full. I thanked my uncle for his help and support. I was so happy to have this truck.

I kept my head focused on work. My free time was filled with visits to the gym or going to the movies. At first, I had the urge to go out to bars and drink or go to dance clubs and party, but after a few weeks of my new routine, I stayed strong. The first weekend was the hardest for me as I sat at home on a Friday night bored and tried to fill my time with watching movies. I stayed home on Saturday nights with the intent to go to church the following morning. I would go to church every free Sunday I had. I prayed and even read from a devotional I had bought.

My money was being saved and I found more constructive things to do with my free time, like cooking. I wanted to replicate some of the meals Mom and Grandma served. Soon I looked up new recipes and I found different ways to prepare food. I kept to myself for the most part and relaxed at home. I became someone who would rather stay home on Saturday nights than stay out late partying.

I especially learned to enjoy the mornings, something I had not done for over a decade. I realized that the people who woke up early were usually the most successful. Early morning people were more motivated and upbeat and I knew this change in routine was healthy for me. I enjoyed this lifestyle and felt I was making the most of my second chance.

I checked in with my parole officer once every few months and on one visit, my parole officer informed me that I had yet to pay my restitution.

"I already paid my lawyer," I said. "She told me she put it in escrow."

"I will check it out and get back to you as soon as I hear anything," he said.

A few days passed and I received a call from my parole officer telling me there was no record of this amount anywhere in escrow. I figured my attorney must have used that money to pay herself for representing me. "Well, she did deserve it. It was my fault for not paying her in the first place," I thought.

The parole officer sighed on the phone. "Well, it's past due and I have to tell the court you have failed to comply with the terms of your parole," he said. "You may be in violation of your parole. Pay the restaurant as soon as you can and get the receipt notarized. Return the document to me and I will pass it to the court."

I immediately called Bill and set up a time and place to pay back the money.

"I need a receipt as well and can you please have it notarized?" I asked.

Bill agreed and once we met, I paid the money back in full. Bill handed me the notarized letter of payment which I immediately gave to my parole officer.

Finally, this matter was over. I paid off the attorney and paid the company their money back. It was another step in the right direction to living a better life.

But, one day at work I was approached by a friendly older man asking, "Hey man, are you Daniel?" I said yes and the man told me he was a bounty hunter and that he had an assignment to pick me up and take me into custody for failure to pay my parole officer.

"I paid my restitution already, it was late though. I gave the notarized letter to my parole officer. This is all a misunderstanding," I said.

"It's probably a clerical error. Once you're detained for a few hours it'll be cleared up and you'll be released," the bounty hunter replied.

I peacefully agreed to go in and clear up the matter.

But once I was in custody however, I was treated like a criminal. I had my fingerprints and picture taken. I was placed in a holding cell with six other inmates. Everyone in there complained about not being guilty. One by one they were called into questioning and eventually, after four long hours, my name was called. I went into a small disorganized office and a police officer asked me a series of questions. I explained the situation and the police officer treated me as though I was lying.

I was brought back into the holding cell. I waited there for another three hours until I was finally put into a separate holding cell. They stripped me down and took my shoes. They handed me an orange jumpsuit and a small paper bag of food. I was in that holding cell for almost five hours, twelve hours total time in the police station. Time seemed to waste away and I could see from the other windows that it was dark outside. The door finally opened and I was told I was being detained overnight.

Around midnight, I was led in handcuffs into another room that looked more like the prison cells on television. There was a small gathering area in the middle and separate cells upstairs and on the main floor. I was led into a room with another inmate and was told to sleep on the empty bed until the next morning. I lay there all night, cold and upset that this was happening. I thought back to that day I drunkenly gambled nine hundred dollars away and I knew that the consequences were not over yet.

The next morning, I woke up for roll call and was led to a small, tasteless breakfast. I had heard warnings about prison food, but I was starving so I ate it all. When breakfast was over, I was led into the same holding cell from the night before, this time with ten other people. It reeked of urine and body odor. I waited in this room quietly until my name was called and I was led to a desk with a lady at a computer. I told her the situation and she typed it into the computer.

"You're actually correct," she said as she clicked through the files on her computer. "So don't worry, you'll be released soon."

I was relived, but mostly annoyed that the process took so long. I was led back into the holding cell until I was discharged. The worst part of this whole experience was the waiting and boredom. The afternoon came and my name was finally called. I was finally free to leave.

Months went by and I was in great shape. My new lifestyle brought about a better diet. I was focused on work and spent my energy learning new tasks and increasing my knowledge of life. I started reading more devotional books and thrived from the wholesome living. I put my past behind me and learned from my new lease on life. God worked in my heart and for the first time, I was keeping my promises.

CALIFORNIA DREAMS

I LIKED BEING ABLE TO keep up to date with my friends and family through social media. Jordan, one of my friends from when I was in school, posted about living in Los Angeles and working in the movie industry with his brother, Joshua. My love for cinema made me want to live in Los Angeles one day and be an actor. I started corresponding with Jordan once a week. I loved hearing Jordan's stories about working on movie sets and dealing with actors. Jordan was a movie producer and Joshua worked as an assistant for one of the most renowned acting coaches in Hollywood. Their family still lived in the Rockville area and during winter break that year they headed back home to visit. Jordan told me that he would stop by the restaurant when he was in town.

I walked around the dining room one night and talked with guests. During a table visit, someone waved me over. Jordan was there with some of his old high school friends. I sat down at the booth and listened as Jordan told stories of actors he worked with and people he had met. I thought it sounded really extraordinary to be a part of this business. I loved my management job, but to be able to do something I had always had a passion for was exciting.

"Okay Jordan, what do I have to do be part of the movie scene?" I asked. "I'm serious about this, to make the move, how much would I have to save? If I went to LA, would I be able to use you as a connection to get proper acting classes and auditions?"

"If you're serious," he said, "then you should save up at least five thousand dollars for the move. Joshua can get you an audition with his boss, Martin. He's the top acting coach in LA. He has developed some of the best in the business. You'll need to find a job with flexible hours, so you are free to go to classes at night and auditions throughout the week."

I had a decision to make. Would I stay in a job that paid very well or journey across the country to pursue my dreams? I knew that if I went for my dream I could one day tell my children to do the same. I also knew that if I wanted to make the move I had to save my money.

From that point forward I did just that. I thought back to several years before when I did not have two pennies to rub together. I also started looking at the costs of living in the Hollywood area.

I found out that my current company had a location within ten miles of where I was looking to rent in the heart of Hollywood. Once I had saved up almost six thousand dollars a few months later, I talked to my boss about the possibility of transferring to the Burbank, California, location, but only as a server so I could have more free time to pursue acting.

"You are crazy," my boss said. "This is a huge life change. I have to say I commend your passion to follow your dreams. I will make all the necessary calls to make it happen for you."

I applied to all three of the apartments I found that were all within the same area. My credit wasn't that good, but I was approved by the cheapest of the three. I geared up for my big move. I still drove the truck I bought from Uncle Eugene. I didn't want to sell the vehicle because it was the best car I ever owned and it represented a special moment for me. Unfortunately, after I calculated the cost to drive to Los Angeles from Maryland, it would be almost a thousand dollars just in gas. I put my truck up for sale and I was able to make a nice profit. I found a Honda Accord that was perfect for me. It was exactly what I needed and it saved me hundreds on gas during the cross-country trek. Jordan and Joshua were excited to hear about my progress for the journey to LA.

Dad was getting remarried at the beginning of April to a woman he had been faithfully dating for over two years. I was asked to be in the wedding, so my trip was planned after the ceremony. I was the best man in my Dad's wedding. Laura, Dad's new wife, was kind and friendly. She loved my dad very much and took good care of him. I was happy that Dad had someone to spend the rest of his life together with. I was also happy I was not leaving Dad alone.

A week before I left, I received a call from my old roommate, Jeff. He had business in St. Louis and heard I was driving to California. Jeff offered to pay for the first leg of the trip if I drove him out to St. Louis. Jeff said he would fly back, but that this would save him money in the long run rather than a round trip flight. I loved the adventure this trip became and looked forward to spending some quality time with Jeff. I planned out my route and figured it would be a three-day drive.

Jeff and I met at Derrick's house in Martinsburg where the trip would start. The night before, the excitement level was high for me since Kevin came over and all four of us guys went out for dinner to celebrate the next journey in my life.

The two woke up early that morning and headed out for the first leg of the trip. It was great having someone to talk to and share the first part of my experience with. Once we got to St. Louis, we checked in at a hotel and went out to eat like gentlemen.

When morning came, I said goodbye to Jeff, packed my overnight bag, and started on the road. I passed through Oklahoma during tornado season which was not something that I took into account when I was planning. On the phone, Derrick updated me about where I was in regard to the huge tornado that was tearing through the state.

"Okay dude, I have been reading online about tornados and here's what you have to do if you see one. Stop your car under a bridge immediately and get out of the vehicle. Then you need to strip down all your clothes and run into an open field for shelter," Derrick said.

I was suspicious. "What? That sounds insane. Pretty sure you might want to fact check the website you're on. If I did that, I think you would just hear on the news of a large dead naked guy that got picked up from the storm and dropped on a house somewhere else," I explained as I smiled.

We both laughed and I knew Derrick was just worried for his friend.

The next stop was Texas. It was dark at this point and I was only on the northern tip of Texas. I saw tumbleweeds and even observed an armadillo crossing the road. I started to cramp from driving but I was determined my next stop for the night would be Albuquerque, New Mexico. I finally arrived late at night in Albuquerque.

The next morning, I stopped for gas and energy drinks and I headed back on the road. I had missed the beautiful scenery of New Mexico during the night as I drove since it was dark. Now I could see the amazing mesas and flat plateaus. The landscape was completely different than West Virginia. After New Mexico came Arizona with its own unique beauty. Some areas were deserts, but then a beautiful oasis was right around the corner. The way the land blended into the clear blue sky was amazing. I thanked God for such a wonderful trip—I sang praises to God for all the provisions He had made for me.

Near the end of my travels through Arizona, I encountered a thing of wonder. I was almost to the California state line. I went up a mountain and saw snow cascading at the peak. The sight was so calming to me and to see so many of God's wonders along this trip blessed my soul.

Finally the moment arrived and I crossed the bridge into California. I rolled my windows down and let the cool breeze blow through my hair. Now I was on the last day of my trip and I was a day early. I decided to stay in a small town outside of Los Angeles. I was filled with excitement and anticipation. I felt like this trip was the first time I was able to be alone with God, away from any distractions. I knew there would be many hurdles in the next few weeks. I came to the decision that I would give Los Angeles one year and once the year ended I would either be headed in a good direction with my acting career or go back home. Either way, I could stand proud that I had followed my dreams.

The next day came and I was anxious to get back on the road and head into Los Angeles. There was no traffic during the entire trip for the last four days. My journey had spanned eleven states and over twenty-six hundred miles. My anticipation was high and I felt at peace during my entire trip. Once I was within the limits of Los Angeles I encountered my first traffic jam. Los Angeles was so busy and no matter where I went I was in bumper-to-bumper traffic. I eventually made it to my exit on the interstate and saw my new apartment. My plan was to pay the landlord and get settled in, then reach out to Jordan and Joshua to meet with them.

The apartment door opened into a small studio. I had never seen this type of studio before—this had only a bedroom and a closet connecting to a full bathroom. There was no kitchen, just a mini fridge. The only sink in the apartment was located in the bathroom. I was so excited to have my own living space that I didn't mind the small apartment.

After the movers left that evening and a full day of errands, I sat back and looked at my fully stocked new apartment. Finally, my room was complete. I had been so busy with moving day that I had not eaten anything. I called up Jordan, and we decided to go to Burbank and eat dinner at the restaurant I was about to work at as a server. The service was slow but the concept was exactly the same as the one I had just come from. Afterward, we both met Joshua and sat at a small dinner table and chatted and drank coffee until late into the night. I found a lot out about the two brothers and what brought them to LA in the first place.

They had lived in Orlando and worked for Disney when Jordan was cast to be in an Oscar Winning movie with Charlize Theron. He didn't even have a speaking role, but I had watched the movie and easily remembered the scenes with Jordan's character. I was excited to be there with Joshua and Jordan—both were genuine, life-long family friends and I looked forward to the next year hanging out with them.

The next day I woke up to the sun shining through my big double windows. The heat from the sun shone down on me and I knew I wouldn't be able to sleep in too often. I opened my blinds and to my delight, I could clearly see the Hollywood sign off in the hills of Los Angeles. This was motivation enough for me every morning to get up and enjoy my new life in LA.

NIGHTMARE

TWO WEEKS WENT BY AND I was ready to start working again. I went to a few auditions to get some experience and I even got headshots done by a local photographer. I hired a booking agent who promised to get me auditions for small roles in television shows and courtroom dramas. I spent most of the money I saved during those two weeks, investing it in what I figured would be my new career. I wrote and performed several character sketches that I posted on YouTube and other similar websites.

I met with Joshua and set up an audition with an acting coach named Martin that Joshua worked for. I performed a scene that was familiar to me and mimicked my life experiences from a small indie movie, *There Will Be Blood*. The character was a young man that preached in a small town and performed his sermons with a great deal of showmanship. The film's portrayal of church reminded me of several of the churches I went to as a child where I felt the pastors faked their faith and speech to build favor from the audience. I practiced the speech several times. I was sure this scene, if done right, would launch me into the classes that would give me the tools I needed to be a real actor. I went to the audition and Martin observed my performance. Martin told me that he liked my ability and how much the classes cost. I was low on finances at that point so I needed to start working before I could start the classes.

I had a job already with the restaurant, but I had yet to call the new store and communicate with them. I wanted to see what else was out there before calling and if there were other serving positions available closer to where I lived.

It was now three weeks since I moved to California, and I still had not started working. I received a call from Chevy's Fresh Mex and set up an appointment to introduce myself.

The next day I went to visit the Chevy's located in Burbank. When I got into my vehicle, I realized I had a ticket. This parking thing was a pain. As soon as I turned onto the main road, the clutch went out on the car and I was stuck in the middle of a traffic jam in the middle of an intersection. The power steering was also out, so I had to manually pull my wheel and drift three blocks back where I started.

I called Chevy's and told them about my situation. They responded that if I couldn't find a way to get there, I should find another place to work. Now I had no job or insurance in this new town. The end of the month was coming and I knew I was not going to have the money for rent. Around this time, too, I was in severe pain from a back molar that had lost its filling. I did not think much about it when it fell out. I had not gone to the dentist in years since I couldn't afford insurance, so I kept the pain under control with pain medication to alleviate the pressure. I even bought a huge bottle of ibuprofen with me on my road trip to LA. I didn't pay attention to how many pills I needed for a given day, but it became normal for me to need three or four pills to get through. So instead of staying at my apartment and worrying about the job and my aching jaw, I decided to get online and job search. I found two locations but quickly realized they were not interested. I got an idea to look for a Buffalo Wild Wings. I figured I could at least get hired as a server. Since it would not be the same location, I would not have to worry about my past legal battles. My lawyer had it expunged from my record months ago.

I looked up the closest location and amazingly enough, it was only two miles from my apartment. I walked to the location and walked into a very familiar scene. Located on Hollywood Boulevard, Buffalo Wild Wings was across the street from Grauman's Chinese Theater. I asked the hostess if the location was currently hiring and she told me they were always accepting applications. There was a work-around for this, however, and I knew it. After I filled out the application, I asked to give it to a manager, knowing that I could get an interview. Sure enough, I met with one of the managers and made sure to wow them with my experience and love of the company. The manager was floored by the amount of enthusiasm I had, but he was especially excited to have the option of having a former general manager working there as a server. I promised that if I was hired, I would do all I could to better the staff and properly execute the mission statement of the company. The floor manager set up a second interview with the bar manager.

I was a day away from my next interview, so I decided to go to the gym. I had received a letter about my late rent and wanted to work off some of my stress. I got off the elliptical and the cord connecting my cell phone to my ear pieces got intertwined in the machine. The elliptical jerked my cell phone and drove it straight to the hard concrete floor. My phone was my entire life—the screen was completely black and shattered. All my phone numbers, emails, and the only internet I had access to was all gone in an instant. I did not know what to do.

Without my phone, I went in for my second interview the next day. The bar manager was very friendly and kind. She was easy to talk to and loved my passion. She said she wished she could hire me right then, but she was worried that there was more to the story than what I was telling them. She wondered how someone with this much knowledge and passion for the company was not still employed. Things weren't adding up for her. She told me she would talk to the management team and call me back for my third interview. I quickly told her about my cell phone issue and that there was no way to reach me. I asked for a chance to sit down with the general manager for my third interview and for a chance to convince him that I was a good investment. She had me wait at the table while she went to talk to the general manager. She came back and told me to return at the end of the next week for my third interview. I knew this would just delay making money to pay rent even more, but I had to do whatever they needed me to do in order to get this job.

I went back to my apartment depressed. I watched the DVDs I'd collected over the last few years to keep my mind off my boredom. I walked to the bank up the street and checked my account. I currently was down to less than a hundred dollars in my account. I had to use this money as sparingly as possible. I bought two loaves of bread, some off-brand peanut butter, and a case of water at the local store before walking home. When I checked on my car, I found three more tickets on the windshield. I had to do something about my car.

I went to a pay phone near the grocery store and called AAA. I got a free tow, and my plan was to move the car to the parking lot of a grocery store until I could figure out what to do. When the tow truck driver arrived, I told him about my situation. The driver asked if I owned the car free and clear. I quickly told him I had the title in hand. The driver said that he had a friend that fixed up old vehicles and sold them, and that he would give him a call. After the call, the tow truck driver said his friend would give me three hundred dollars for the car. I eagerly accepted the offer.

At the end of the next week, I dressed up and went for my third interview. I met the general manager, a mild-mannered older man, who seemed to look for any way to refuse the job to me. I had conducted hundreds of interviews throughout my career, so I acquired the ability to read people well. Since I needed this job desperately, I wasn't going to give the general manager an opportunity to say no. I spoke clearly and precisely. I was enthusiastic and friendly. I never mentioned any of my financial troubles because I knew that usually meant the interviewee was willing to break the rules in order make extra money. I impressed the general manager so much that he wanted to hire me right then. The only problem was that he was not certain of my past with the company. He told me that he wanted me to sit down with the regional manager and that he was going to let him decide on my employment, but that the regional manager wasn't coming to their location for two weeks. The meeting would have to be postponed. I knew the meeting was my only option at this point and that I had no other choice but to wait. Deflated and depressed, I left the store.

Instead of going home, I decided to stop at the studio where Joshua and Martin worked, since it was on my way back home. When I arrived, Joshua was finishing up with a meeting. He welcomed me with open arms and brought me into his office. I sat down and unloaded the situation to Joshua. I had lived in Los Angeles for almost two months at this point and was getting eaten alive. I even told Joshua about my cell phone being destroyed and having no way to communicate.

Joshua's heart went out to me. Joshua left his office and came back five minutes later. He was holding a red cell phone.

"Martin has an extra cell phone he's not using. Use this as a way to communicate with the job and your family until you get yourself situated. Honestly though Dan, you have to look at other job options, because maybe this job is not God's will," Joshua said.

Joshua's act of kindness meant the world to me. I left the studio and went back to Buffalo Wild Wings. I gave the general manager my new number so I could be reached if any plans changed. I called Dad so that he would know I was okay. Things were looking brighter.

The day of my fourth interview, there was a knock at the door. A man handed me a manila envelope with a series of documents stating that I had sixty days to pay my current and past rent, along with other fees. It totaled over two thousand dollars. I knew that everything rode on this interview.

I received a call from Joshua right before I left the apartment. Joshua worked with many prominent actors, and often talked to them before auditions to calm them down. This time was no different, and Joshua gave a speech one could expect from *Remember the Titans*; it was beautiful and completely put me in control of my upcoming meeting.

I went into the meeting with an air of confidence. The regional manager sat down with me and right away got into the reasons I was no longer with the company on the East Coast. I explained the events that led to my termination and told the manager I was working hard to better my name and even stated I could provide many references from team members within the current management team from the East Coast locations. The regional manager was very interested in talking with them. I provided three names and phone numbers of people still employed in high places within the company. He told me he would talk to the references over the next week and let me know his decision. I was left waiting once again.

That night, my tooth bothered me immensely. I was now up to four pills, three times a day. I had an intense shooting pain in my mouth and no matter how many pills I took, the pain was still present. It was so bad I could not fall asleep. At five in the morning, I finally passed out from sheer exhaustion. I woke up and was not able to open my mouth. My jaw was swollen shut. I looked up the symptoms I experienced and found out I had lockjaw, caused by an abscessed tooth. My tooth was exposed so much during the last five months that it caused complete decay. I read that it could quickly get into the bloodstream and cause death. I freaked out and called Jordan and asked him to drive me to the hospital. Jordan couldn't since he was out of town and Joshua was not answering his phone because he was on a movie set. I called 911. I rode in an ambulance to the hospital and asked for them to remove the tooth. They could not perform oral surgery, but they gave me Fentanyl for my pain. The nurses started by giving me a quadruple shot and told me to lay still and that in a few minutes I shouldn't feel the pain anymore. After fifteen minutes, my legs and arms were numb but I still felt my throbbing tooth. They gave me another double shot of the strongest pain medicine they had. I walked around the waiting room and hoped it would accelerate the medication. I felt the medicine hit me like a ton of bricks. My entire body went numb and I felt like I was walking on a ship at sea since I could no longer walk straight. Even though my whole body was feeling the effects of the medication, the throbbing in my mouth was still pulsating through my entire head. I asked the doctors what to do and they told me that without insurance, they could not do anything else and that I was discharged to go. I was six or seven blocks from my apartment and could barely even stand up straight. I stumbled out the front door of the emergency room and tried to gather myself. I tried to walk home, but I felt like I was drunk and walked almost sideways down the street.

I finally made it safely to my apartment and passed out from the medication. I woke up and decided to try and find some remedies for the pain online. I read that I needed to get rid of the infection before I could have any type of surgery. But, since I didn't have insurance, I couldn't afford to see a dentist.

I finally called Dad and asked him for help. Dad was not employed so he had no money to help me but he suggested calling Grandma. I knew that ever since I moved to California, my family had been pressuring Grandma to sell her house and move in with my aunt. I talked to Grandma and found out that other family members tried to cash in on her recent sale and tried to borrow money from her. Dad was one of those people. I did not want to ask Grandma, but I knew she would help me. Grandma wanted to help me out, but she was tired of everyone coming to her for money. I knew there was no one else I could go to and I felt terrible. She hesitantly agreed to help.

I went to a dentist I found online that seemed inexpensive and once the dentist saw my mouth, he told me I needed to take antibiotics for a week before going to an oral surgeon to have the tooth extracted. I was disappointed about the delay and was already in so much pain that I started to cry. The dentist felt sorry for me because he knew I did not have insurance. He suggested that I call the school of dentistry at the UCLA campus since they do simple surgeries like this and since it is done by students, they charge only a portion of the cost of an oral surgeon. He wrote a prescription for pain medicine and antibiotics and sent me home.

After a long week of taking the antibiotic, I went to the UCLA School of Dentistry and signed the paperwork for the surgery. While in the waiting room, I received a call from an unknown number. I could barely talk but I answered anyway. It was the regional manager from Buffalo Wild Wings. He said he called all of my references and checked with the corporate offices, and that I was cleared for hire. I was ecstatic, thanking the manager for the call and for the opportunity. I realized my start date gave me plenty of time to recover from the surgery.

The operation was complete and my tooth was removed. The surgery was only forty dollars, and Grandma was happy to help me out with payment. My mouth was completely numb and I had to change my gauze every half hour. That night, I thanked God for helping me get my tooth removed and for providing an opportunity to work for my former company again. I asked God to speak to me during these trials and the only response God gave me was, "Be still and know that I am God." I did not understand why this verse was such a constant in my life, but it was the one God reminded me of during tough times.

The night before I started my new job, I was invited to go out to eat with Joshua. Joshua was such an encouragement through all the struggles I had already faced. He took me to a bookstore and bought me a book, *The Birthright: Out of the Servant's Quarters Into the Father's House* by John Sheasby. Joshua challenged me to read the book and discuss it with him after. Joshua told me about his own struggles he faced during his childhood and early adult life. Joshua grew up in a strict Baptist church and always felt like no matter what he did, it was never good enough for God. Anger and resentment was something that Joshua carried for many years. He came across this particular author and speaker and was floored by the words of encouragement and hope he spoke. This book helped open Joshua's eyes to the power of forgiveness, not just God's forgiveness to mankind, but that there is freedom in forgiveness among ourselves, too. I was interested in the book since I had many people I held resentment toward, including myself and the Lord. Maybe it was time to start uncovering my anger and start moving on.

During the next few months I worked on forgiving all those against whom I held bitterness. My first challenge was forgiving my dad. I looked up to Dad my entire adolescent years, but after Mom passed, I saw Dad display his humanness. I prayed for God to give me strength to fully forgive my dad. I called Dad one night and had a conversation that lasted several hours. I told him that I forgave him and that I was going to support him from this point forward. Tears were shed on both ends of the phone, and that moment helped build my relationship again with my dad.

I also spent some time in prayer and asked for forgiveness from God for holding resentment toward Him for taking Mom. I wept on my knees while I thanked God for forgiving me for all the anger I had held for all those years. I was so thankful for Joshua's gift and the Spirit's prompting since I was making amends to all the people I had held grudges to for so long. I started to experience the true freedom of forgiveness—a peace that would not have been possible with my own doing.

The first day of my new job with Buffalo Wild Wings was upon me. I had less than five weeks to make over three thousand dollars or I would be evicted from my apartment. The pressure was mounting. The first day was filled with orientation, paperwork, and safety videos. I remembered when those safety videos were first released.

I worked the rest of the week and followed team members while they served tables. Within a few days, I was promoted to my own tables. My first shifts were during the daytime hours, but I still managed to make seventy to eighty dollars. I paid close attention to the management team when they wrote the night floor plan. I asked if they had enough servers and if they were short, I offered to stay and work a double shift. During the first week,

I saved seven hundred dollars. I knew that was a good start, but I had to do even better.

The second week, I continued the same pattern. There was a big game one night and the management asked me if I could work as a barback, or the assistant for the bartender. I told them I was willing to do whatever they needed. That night, I tipped out from the bartenders and collected a hundred dollars. The second week ended and I saved nine hundred dollars. I was over halfway there with only two weeks left to make my rent.

The third week came and went and I saved another seven hundred dollars. I had only one week remaining. The fourth week business was slower than normal. I worked double shifts, took on bigger sections, and even picked up shifts when other servers didn't want them. I finished the week with only six hundred fifty-five dollars. I was short by forty-five dollars. I didn't know what to do and went home disappointed—I had tried so hard to make enough money, just to fall short at the end.

I walked by a lottery ticket store, and even though I never played the lottery, I wanted to spend five dollars on a ticket. I went inside and bought one five-dollar scratch off ticket. I scratched the ticket with my keys and won fifty dollars. I now had enough money to pay my rent. I knew that I was not supposed to play the lottery or rely on a game of chance to pay my rent, but I knew God provided the rest of the money in the most unconventional way.

I continued working and I was determined to save as much money as I could. I saved enough to get a new phone and once I bought it, I went straight to Joshua's studio and handed Martin his phone back. I thanked him with a card I bought at the store and included enough money to pay for the two months of payments while I had used the phone.

I worked very hard at the restaurant and quickly moved into a bartending position. Since I had so much experience as a bar manager in the past, I helped with orders and inventories. I also trained other bartenders that were just starting out. I made my own schedule, and since I worked the bar area by myself during the daytime, I worked every day shift during the week and I worked on the weekends if there were big games. I averaged about seven hundred dollars a week from tips alone.

It was the end of the summer of 2012 and fall was headed our way. I had been in LA for almost six months and I still had not made any steps toward my acting goals. I had told myself before driving out that if I had not made any headway in my acting career in a year that I would move back to West Virginia.

But, despite the six-month set back, I was finally financially stable enough to focus on my acting career. I went to auditions when I could, even though I stayed busy working as a bartender. Since I didn't have a vehicle, I was limited to places that were within walking distance or close to the metro. I often observed the people on the metro when I was waiting for my stop. Many people had sad looks on their faces and I wondered what their stories were. When I walked to work on Hollywood Boulevard, there were crowds of people dressed in superhero and cartoon character costumes that charged money to tourists to take pictures with them. Sometimes there were street performers who played on upside down buckets like a drum set, or a man spray painted in silver or gold acting like a statue that danced once someone paid him.

In January 2013, with no luck so far with my acting dreams, I found out that there was a film company coming in to the restaurant to film a series of training videos for Buffalo Wild Wings. If these training videos were good, they would be aired in every Buffalo Wild Wings location, including the locations I had previously worked. The film crew took a liking to me and I was hired to be the "friendly neighborhood bartender" in the video. I did not get paid for my acting, but it was a great opportunity nonetheless. Every week they filmed another training video and I got to deliver several lines. It became something I looked forward to since it made up for the flopped year in LA.

One evening as I got home from work, Jordan called. He was producing a movie and was filming at Air Hollywood, a studio set that was famous for filming movies such as *Airplane!*, *Flight*, and *Soul Plane*. Jordan needed help in the art department building items they needed for a specific scene and he needed extra hands to help move set pieces around in-between takes. I was thrilled to be part of this experience and to be on a real live movie set. Jordan picked me up early the next morning and brought me to the studio. I walked inside and saw two airplanes shelled out for movie scenes. I spent the day building set pieces and moving props back and forth. I got to see the way the director watched the scene as it was being filmed and even helped with practical special effects for some of the scenes. The actors that were involved had good conversations with me and I got to observe some of the extras' behavior. They acted one way in the presence of the talented actors and another when they were not around. I saw through their pretense and noticed it more and more.

Over the next two months, I noticed how people treated Jordan whenever we went out. As childhood friends of Joshua and Jordan, I had a real love for them. I noticed that when people found out that Jordan was a movie producer, they instantly sucked up to him. They did whatever they could to make Jordan feel important, and I saw that this also made Jordan feel special. I knew Jordan was talented and had a ton of special qualities, but I hated how fake actors were around him. I warned Jordan of the fakeness of some of the people that hung out with him, but I knew I was just coming off as jealous in Jordan's eye. I missed my home and knew that even though the people in Maryland and West Virginia might be a little harder to get along with, they weren't fake. If someone did not like you, they let you know. I was not impressed with the selfish shallowness of Hollywood, and it made me miss home even more.

COMING HOME

IT WAS APRIL AND I finished my first year in Los Angeles. I missed home but even more, my family.

I spent most of my time reading books about forgiveness and trying to make amends with people I wronged in the past. I talked with family members I hurt or that I held resentment toward. I forgave Alicia for the way she had manipulated my heart. I forgave Damon for trying to pin me with the theft from the ATMs. I was able to forgive and forget anyone who ever wronged me, but I had yet to forgive myself.

I studied the Bible and started to study the reason that the verse in Psalms kept coming up in my life; "Be still and know that I am God." I realized something—the verse meant that we tend to try to do everything on our own. We think that we are in control of our own life and many times forget about God when things are going in our own favor. We tend to look to God only when we are stuck in despair. I had put so much planning and thought into moving to LA. I had prepared and made provisions for myself to make the trip. I had thought that acting was my dream. But when I arrived, a series of events that were completely out of my control started to happen. I wrecked my car, all of my money was gone, I lost the job I had set up for myself, I almost lost my apartment because I was behind three months on rent, and I even had an abscessed tooth that became life threatening. All these problems were unseen before I moved. These problems almost destroyed me, but in the midst of my troubles God was in control of my life and made provisions that were out of my control to save me. I needed to stop trying to do things on my own, and be still and let God take control of my life. God's way offered peace and soundness of mind, while my way led to depression and constant frustration.

I also learned during this time of reflection that my dream of acting was not what it seemed. I saw the way that the love of money and fame caused people to be fake and self-absorbed. I realized that Hollywood became, at least in my mind, a dwelling home of atheists. I watched movies and television with a different viewpoint now, and actually listened and heard the words people spoke. Many times comedians bashed the faith and hope of my Lord. I saw through the arrogance and pride that people projected, and instead saw their emptiness and sorrow. I realized that once I saw behind the camera lens of Hollywood, there were millions of lost dreams and empty souls. Now when I saw the homeless on Hollywood streets, I saw the hope they once had by moving to LA with dreams of success and riches only to be eaten alive by this town and left to rot on the streets as a reminder to others. I was ready to leave. I came to learn how to act, but what I learned from my Savior was the truth.

I packed my things into five cardboard boxes and Joshua drove me to the post office to mail them back home. I gave friends my TV as well as other big items that were too heavy or fragile to ship across the country. I talked to Derrick, and he offered me a place to stay for a few weeks while I looked for a job. I bought a one-way plane ticket back home and Joshua drove me to the airport to see me off. I loved the time I spent with Joshua, Jordan, and Martin. They had become family to me.

When I landed in the airport, Derrick greeted me at the terminal with open arms. Derrick and I embraced in a tight hug. Derrick drove me back to his house, and later that night Kevin came over and hung out and heard stories of my adventures. The next night I heard that my dad and Laura were going to be in Martinsburg, stopping at a buffet restaurant with Laura's class. She was a music teacher and was on a band trip for a school competition. I told Dad that Derrick was going to meet him and give him something. I hadn't told Dad I was back in town, so this was going to be a fun surprise.

When the bus arrived in the parking lot, Derrick and I were in the car waiting. Derrick went out first and met with Dad. I quietly snuck behind some cars and walked up behind Dad. I embraced him with a big hug and Dad was in shock. He was so thankful to have his son back home. Laura was with the students, but when she smiled her eyes were filled with tears of joy. She knew how much that meant to her husband.

The next day I called Grandma and found that she had recently come to visit the family, too—she was staying with my aunt and uncle. I went to the house and we sat and talked for hours and shared stories. Grandma seemed much happier than she was this time last year. I asked her why she was so happy and she told me that she went to her high school reunion a few months ago and even though there were only a handful of classmates still alive from her class, one man in particular was thrilled to see her. Sam lost his wife about the same time Grandma lost Grandpa They sat and talked the entire dinner and Sam admitted he had always been attracted to her. Sam talked to Grandma on the phone for the last few months and they became close. They made the decision to start dating and Grandma was so happy. She reminded me of a high school girl that had a crush on a boy. That night, I met Sam and I saw how happy Sam made her. I knew how hard it was for her after Grandpa passed. I knew she still loved Grandpa forever, but that Sam had breathed new life into her. I watched as Grandma reached for Sam's hand and giggled like a schoolgirl. I loved to see her happy again.

I began to wear out my welcome at Derrick and Tammy's house. It had been several weeks and I felt bad for intruding. But it wasn't long before I saved some money, bought a car, and found out that Kevin had a couch that folded into a bed. I asked Kevin if I could move in. Kevin had a roommate at the time, but both of them did not mind. Within a few months of sleeping on

Kevin's couch, the roommate got a job offer in another town and moved out. I moved into the room I lived in years before.

Unfortunately for me, Kevin started dating a girl named Katherine. She came over more and more, and I spent my nights barricaded in my room to give them their privacy. Kevin thought about moving into a bigger apartment, so he searched for a new place to live. It didn't take long before Kevin and I moved into a new, bigger apartment in Martinsburg. It had a deck, side room, and we each had our own bathroom. I knew this bigger apartment meant higher rent. I had to find a job as soon as I could.

GROWING PAINS

I GOT A CALL FROM Derrick one day that Tammy found an interesting job listing for "role players." I had no idea what that was but the pay seemed very good. I applied and went for an interview. I quickly found out this job was for the Department of State. All year long diplomats, government agents, and representatives were tasked with overseas missions. They often found themselves in high risk areas. The Department of State held interactive training classes to help train these individuals on what to do when faced with a hostile situation. That was where the role players came in. They acted as characters in hostile environments to help equip the individual. The better a role player acted, the more prepared the representative was when actually faced with similar situations overseas. I was thrilled with the chance to use my acting in this type of environment. I got dressed up, used an accent, and even tried to get under the skin of the trainees. I found a job I absolutely loved, and the fact that I was helping people prepare for hostile elements overseas was a bonus.

I thrived in my first few weekends as a role player. I was involved in two separate scenarios, and they ran through the scenarios for two different training classes. The afternoon scenario was my favorite. I was the head guard of a refugee camp. I used a stick or even a toothpick as a prop to make myself look more like an arrogant leader. The other guards followed my lead, and they harassed the trainees while the teachers watched. I talked in an accent I thought of as a type of *Borat* meets *Zohan*, even though people often told me I sounded Russian. I got to pretend to be someone else: a cocky, pretentious jerk. I watched to see if someone was taking the exercise lightly and got in his face and yelled at him. I looked for cues that were not correct according to the training, and then verbally attacked them. I knew not to touch the trainees, but I loved it when I tested the patience of someone who was hot headed. At the end of each scenario, I gave my feedback to the trainers on how the people did. I was finally doing something I was passionate about, and I didn't have to be in LA to do it.

I worked as a role player only one day each week. The rest of the week, the representatives were in the classroom for training. Even though this job paid extremely well for working only once a week, I still needed a second job for the rest of the time. Since I was burnt out from my time in the restaurant business, I was determined to find another career.

During this time of job searching, I enjoyed my time with Kevin and Katherine, but I longed for someone to spend my personal time with. I wished I could find a girl that I could connect with both mentally and spiritually. I had heard about a few dating apps and built profiles for several of them. I chatted with many different girls and eventually met them in person on a date. I enjoyed having more of a social life, but I just could not find a true connection.

That changed when I started a conversation with one girl, Allison, who had an interesting profile on Tinder. She claimed to be a world traveler and had many pictures on her profile of hiking and exploring different locations. Allison was friendly and had a sweet and innocent demeanor. She was extremely attractive with long brown hair and blonde highlights. I really enjoyed chatting with her online. She said in her profile that she was a basketball coach, so I asked her if she was also a basketball fan. She said she was, and that really piqued my interest. I finally asked her on a date since I felt like I knew as much about her as I could without meeting her in person. She accepted, and we scheduled our first date.

I almost canceled the date. I remembered all the failed dating attempts in my past and was felt reluctant to try again. But I went back and read the conversations I'd had with Allison and decided to go on the date anyway. I met her at a sports restaurant in Hagerstown. She arrived late, and I was nervous. When she got out of her nice vehicle, my first impression was that Allison was well-dressed with long, beautiful hair. She had the most intriguing eyes. She presented herself in a proper and almost standoffish manner—she was nervous as well. When we sat down, I started the conversation by asking Allison lots of sports related questions to break the ice.

"So you like basketball. Do you like any other sports?" I asked.

Allison perked up. "I love football. Miami Dolphins are my team! What team do you follow?"

I sat back, laughed and replied, "I am a New England Patriots fan! Mostly because of Tom Brady, but I love their team aspect. So, the Dolphins, huh, guess I don't have to worry about you being a bandwagon fan."

I noticed my comment did not go over well with Allison. She was clearly much more of a football fan than I was, so I quickly dropped the subject.

My faith was important to me, so I really needed to find out about her beliefs.

"So Allison, this may be a deal breaker, but I'm a Christian. Do you go to church? If so, what would you consider yourself to be?" I asked. I knew this was a bold question, but I wanted to make sure I was up front with her about my stand.

"I'm a Christian as well. I go to church every Sunday with my family. My faith is very important to me," she said.

I thought to myself, "This girl is perfect for me! I could really see myself in a real relationship with her."

We sat at the table for a few hours, talking and sharing stories. I felt great about how the date was going, as she had this uncanny ability to keep me alert and focused. Every so often she revealed a gentle side. I really liked Allison, but I knew Allison was leaving town to London at the end of the week to see the Dolphins play a game.

"This girl must know how to save her money!" I thought. Frugality was another good quality I appreciated. Her trip sparked many questions for me.

"Was she going to be headed to London alone?" I thought. "Was Allison a girl who was sincere, or would I be led on just to have my heart broken?"

When dinner was over I walked Allison out of the restaurant to her vehicle. We talked in the chilly autumn night for a few minutes and I went to give Allison a hug goodbye. As we hugged, I felt Allison turn her head toward me. We locked eyes and I went in for a kiss. I was shocked by what an incredible kisser she was.

We stood in the parking lot for what seemed like hours holding each other, talking, and kissing. When we kissed, I got a glimpse of her sweet and beautiful face. I really wanted to date this girl. The connection was not just physical attraction, it was emotional and spiritual. I left that night excited for what the future held.

I texted Allison a few times the next day, but after a few texts the conversation grew small. I told her to enjoy her trip and to reach out to me when she got back. I figured if it was meant to be then we would surely connect again.

Two weeks passed and I had not heard from Allison. I thought that it must not have been meant to happen. I set up a few dates with other girls I met online and went on several first dates, but I did not feel any connections. The girls I met were either not Christian, or I lost interest in them quickly.

Over the next few months, I spent most of my time working small jobs and going out with girls so I was not at home very often. Kevin's girlfriend, Katherine, moved in with us. The walls were so thin that I practically heard every conversation they had, much to my displeasure. I stayed confined to my room and tried to give them space. I became quite the hermit. I was miserable and finally decided to move out and find my own place. When the end of the lease came, I temporarily moved in with my Aunt Jenica until I found my own place. I offered to pay her some money while I stayed on her couch, but she told me not to worry about it and to save my money. I wanted to help in some way, so I assisted her with special projects around the house that needed to be completed. In the morning, I would wake up to the smell of coffee from Aunt

Jenica's kitchen and sit and talk with her for hours about life and my goals. I appreciated this time with her. Whenever I was at the store, I called her to see if she needed any items.

At night, I would lay on the couch in the living room alone and chat with girls online. I had multiple dates lined up with different girls from around the area but I kept delaying the dates because in my heart, I really wanted to settle down. I started going to church again and spent time in prayer and read the Bible. I remembered that when I was younger Mom told me to pray for God to send a wife that was perfect for me. I thought it was a good idea to start this prayer again since I felt like I was at a point in my life where I was ready to settle down. I yearned to connect with a special woman.

GIFT FROM GOD

GOD'S TIMING IS ALWAYS THE best and when I prayed for something, I needed to be prepared for God to answer. Within one day of praying for God to send me my wife, I received a message on Tinder from Allison. Allison and I started out with small talk and once we broke the ice, I jokingly asked her why she blew me off six months earlier. The conversation went well, so I asked if I was ever going to get a second date. Allison evaded the question in a flirtatious manner. She told me I needed to prove myself to her before she would give me another date.

I still debated about going on dates with a few other girls at this point. The next morning, I talked with Aunt Jenica over our coffee. I told her I was having girl problems and she asked what was wrong.

"Well Aunt Jen, here's the issue. I have been using Tinder and other dating apps for some time now. I have four or five girls I could go out with, but I am so tired of the dating scene that I just wish I could find one special girl and settle down," I explained. Aunt Jenica sat back shocked.

"Okay, Dan, let's do a test. List the characteristics you look for in the right woman," she challenged.

"I want someone I find attractive, intelligent, someone to talk to, and someone who shares the same faith as me," I answered.

"Now describe in detail the girls you are currently talking to and considering dating," she said.

I spent the next hour describing the list of qualities for each woman I had connected with online. I finished with mentioning Allison.

Aunt Jenica looked at me, amused. "Come on, buddy, I thought you were smarter than this. You already know who you need to go after."

I curiously looked at Aunt Jenica. "Who is the one that I should go for?"

She laughed and leaned in toward him. "Allison, silly. You need to forget the rest of the girls and focus all of your energy on her. All of the other girls sound like they have too much baggage for you, and from someone who has lived longer than you, they sound like trouble. Allison sounds perfect for who you are and what you want."

After some thought and more conversations, I agreed.

I went down the street and searched for apartments. I came across the apartment building that DJ lived in over a decade ago. I went to the office and asked them for an application. I filled it out and turned it back in right away. I learned it would be a while until a place opened up, but when one became available I would be contacted.

I went back to Aunt Jenica's house hopeful that God would take care of my housing. I prayed again for God to provide an opportunity to meet with Allison, but only if it was meant to happen. That night, I reached out to Allison and she seemed sad and upset. I asked her what was wrong and she told me that she was betrayed by one of her work friends. She cried on the phone, feeling deceived from her friend. My heart went out to her and I tried to encourage her and lift her spirits. Allison was encouraged by my compassion and told me that she decided to give me another chance. I quickly asked her to dinner that Friday and she agreed to meet me. I was so thankful to God for this chance and prayed that if she was not the one that I should pursue, that future dates would fall through.

Friday came, and Allison and I were still set to meet. We met at a nice Italian restaurant and sat down in a busy dining room. Allison was as beautiful as I remembered. She composed herself in a professional manner and her eyes were mesmerizing. I felt butterflies in my stomach for the first time in a long time. Dinner went well but it was over fast. I walked Allison out to her car and we awkwardly looked at each other and waited for the other one to make a move. I noticed that Allison was much more apprehensive during this date and I felt that if we left each other right now, I might have to wait another six months to get another date. We heard music coming from another restaurant nearby. There was a live band playing and I made the suggestion to go to the restaurant, have dessert, and have more time to talk.

We walked into the packed restaurant with wall-to-wall people laughing and dancing to the band. It was really loud and hard to hear as we talked. I had trouble even holding a conversation with Allison in that atmosphere, so we did not stay very long. As we walked back out to our vehicles, I wanted to kiss her again. I thought that it was not going to happen, but then Allison asked me for a hug. I reached in for a hug and our eyes instantly connected.

We embraced with a tender kiss.

"I thought you were going to leave without kissing me," she said.

"Oh, I wanted to. I just didn't want to make you feel uncomfortable," I told her.

We stood outside for three hours in the chilly April night holding each other, talking and laughing.

I felt led by the Lord to share with Allison my intention to date her with the goal of marriage. I thought that this would scare her away from me, and I had never said this to anyone I had ever dated before. But even though I was hesitant, I revealed my intentions and motives to Allison.

To my bewilderment and delight, she agreed that she was also ready for a relationship. God sent me a woman who was ready for a commitment and He had prepared me to settle down.

The next day, I worked with some friends to do some renovations on their house for some extra money. I spent the day cleaning up the landscaping and painting the trim around their house. When a free chance arose, I texted Allison. She was all I could think about and we made plans to see each other later that evening. Allison lived about an hour away from where I lived. We decided to meet in Hagerstown, which was almost halfway between our homes. I came up with the idea to meet at the bowling alley in Hagerstown, and as soon as we saw each other, we embraced in a hug and kissed.

The next morning, the leasing office called and woke me up. The applicant that was supposed to move into the apartment I visited had backed out, and since I was next on the waiting list, they offered me the apartment. I quickly got my money together and paid the leasing office. I signed a one-year lease and got the keys to my new place. When I called Allison right away and told her the good news, she rejoiced with me. We made plans to have dinner that weekend at the new apartment once I moved myself into the complex. After settling in with some family-donated furniture and cookware, I spent my evening reading my Bible and devotionals. I realized that the Lord had provided for me again. Even though I was faced with uncertainty, I found an apartment of my own, a woman that I wanted a relationship with, and had a job I loved. I got ready for my role-playing job, and knew I had to come home quickly to prepare the special dinner for Allison.

Over the next few weeks, Allison and I took turns visiting each other. In the first month I introduced Allison to Dad and Laura. They both loved her immediately and thought we were perfect together. A few weeks after meeting my parents, Allison prepared me to meet her family. I planned to meet Allison's parents for dinner but on the way there, my car overheated.

"What a great first impression I'm making on her family!" I thought as I walked in late. Despite the embarrassing story, I quickly made friends with Allison's parents.

Our relationship grew stronger with each passing day. We spent our evenings on the phone with each other talking and sharing our life stories. We attended the other's church on the weekends and spent time talking about our faith. During one date, Allison and I decided to go to a bookstore. We went to the faith section, and we found a book that we could use as a devotional together. We did a devotion together every evening, and our relationship as a couple grew even more as our faith grew stronger.

Every week I applied for dozens of jobs to find something I could do during the week. I loved the role-playing job and I did not want to stop working there, but I needed something more stable.

The summer was almost over and I needed to find a job soon or I could lose my apartment. Allison tried to cheer me up, but I felt quite depressed. With life there were always highs and lows, and I strongly believe that without the lows you can not appreciate the highs. With no jobs in sight, I became very nervous. I did the only thing I could do: trust the Lord that He would provide.

Allison called one day and had some news to share. She searched online for jobs and found Primanti Brothers that was preparing to expand across the East Coast. Primanti Brothers was looking for managers to help open new restaurants in the Hagerstown area. I researched the company and found that they had made a name for themselves after being showcased on a popular food television show. The company also relied heavily on sports to draw in business, which fit well with my job background. I applied for the job that day, called Allison, and we prayed that if it was God's will He would provide this job for me.

I spent the next several days anxiously waiting by the phone. It reminded me of when I waited by the phone for a job in LA. I remembered God's simple words of encouragement then: "Be still and know that I am God." I finally received a phone call from Chang, the regional director with the Primanti Brothers. I talked to him on the phone for about an hour and liked his straightforward approach. Chang told me to come to York, Pennsylvania, for an interview, and I could spend a few hours at the location to see if this company was a good fit.

When I reached the store, Chang greeted me and gave me a tour of the restaurant. Chang asked me to work with the team for a few hours and see what

I thought. I felt awkward at first, but I wanted to make a good impression. I learned the table numbers within minutes and worked as a food runner. Since I dressed well for the interview, I knew the guests thought I was a manager. I learned the names of the team members quickly and built relationships seamlessly. After a few hours the lunch rush was over and I sat down with Chang to discuss my day. Chang liked me, but he was not sure why I had carried so many jobs during my career. I tried to explain my reasons as best as I could.

"But I don't understand. Why did you go from being a general manager to working numerous jobs that lasted a year at most?" Chang asked.

"I was let go because of negligence," I said, embarrassed to tell him what really happened.

After several conversations and phone calls that lasted weeks, I felt convicted to tell Chang the truth. I respected Chang and I knew that I could not begin my new job on a dishonest claim. Thankfully, Chang called me in the middle of a movie date with Allison and offered me the job.

"You'll start your training next week in State College. We've booked a hotel room for five nights for you. Feel free to travel back home on your days off," Chang explained.

"Thank you so much," I said. "I look forward to this new opportunity!"

THE HEART OF THE PROBLEM

I WAS READY TO WORK for the new company and I always enjoyed the anticipation of starting a new job. At this point in my life, this was common place for me. I arrived early to the training location and met with Chang.

I still relied on energy drinks and coffee to help boost my energy and I knew I was going to be working in a high-stress environment. I was also aware of a new legal pill called Phenibut. I bought it on the internet and it caused me to be extremely calm in tense situations and it caused my dopamine levels to rise and induced good moods behavior. I discovered that if I took Phenibut in the morning with a pre-workout mix, I would have energy throughout the day and could be calm and happy instead of jittery and stressed. It was the closest thing to street drugs I had ever used. Derrick looked up the side effects of Phenibut and warned me that it was highly addictive and not healthy for someone to take it long-term. I needed to cycle my usage and use it only when it was really needed.

During training, I became stressed quite easily. I had not worked in a high-stress job for a while, and I found myself becoming agitated faster than ever. I did not want to rely on a pill with damaging side effects, so I pushed through the first four days and took Phenibut only on the last day of training.

When my training was complete, I was assigned to work in a closed-down bank building as a hiring location for the new restaurant opening in Hagerstown. I no longer had to commute so far to work and I enjoyed that aspect. I spent the day working in the deconstructed bank holding interviews and hiring staff members.

While Chang appeared competent and professional during the interview, I grew cautious of him quickly because he reminded me of my old boss, Damon. Chang did not handle stress well and many times took his pressures out on the management team. He never seemed to be positive, and constantly complained about everything. The harder I worked, the more it seemed Chang unloaded his negativity on me.

Allison was a bright light during this time. She was a constant loving and caring person that I leaned on heavily for emotional comfort and support. We still read our devotions together and spent hours on the phone with each other nightly. I loved Allison with all of my heart, and I knew that God had sent her to me.

I told Allison about my pre-workout mixes and occasional Phenibut use. She worried greatly for my long-term health while taking these pills and mixes. Allison was the type of person who woke up in the morning and was ready for the day. She did not even drink coffee and I wished I could be more like her. I knew that the constant jittery feeling I had throughout the day was a result of these bad habits. I got used to waking up exhausted every morning and not being able to function until I drank some coffee and started my daily routine of mixes. Allison yearned for me to stop the mixes and Phenibut, but I simply argued that I was fine and that it was completely legal.

It was training time for the staff of the new location and I geared up for the stressful opening. I brought my coffee maker into the office so the management team could keep a steady supply of caffeine in their systems throughout the day. We were spending twelve to fourteen hours a day at work and needed as much energy as possible. The York location needed me to work a shift at their restaurant location on my last work day of the week. I hated to travel, but it was nice to get away from the stress.

I traveled to York and drank my usual mixture of pre-workout mix plus a Phenibut to make the day go quicker. I was anxious for the day to be over so that I could see Allison and spend the weekend with her. I had a dentist appointment scheduled for Monday, but other than that, I had a whole weekend to plan with Allison. The York location was busy that night, and I felt the effects of the Phenibut. I was friendly and talkative, but I left that night feeling exhausted as the mixes wore off.

When I reached Allison's house, my chest was pounding like a drum. When Allison saw me, she immediately suggested that we go to the Emergency Room. I reluctantly agreed since the pain was so intense, I knew I had to do something.

Expecting to leave the ER after a quick check-up, I was mentally planning the weekend with Allison when a nurse came in to take my blood pressure. She immediately noticed something was wrong. She left the room and brought in another nurse to verify her findings. The doctor came in and made me lay down and told me I was in Atrial Fibrillation, a-fib for short. A-fib is when someone has an irregular heartbeat, where one or more valves of the heart are not in rhythm. This can be extremely damaging to my heart if overworked in this fashion. I needed to stay overnight for observation to find the cause of my arrhythmia. I was immediately stressed as I remembered that Mom died from a heart condition.

I stayed in the hospital overnight and was under constant watchful eye from the nurses and doctors. The next morning I was released and Allison took me home. I was tired of being poked all night long by the nurses as they took blood from me every few hours. Allison went to bed that evening but kept a close eye on me. When I woke up the next morning, I had severe pain in my stomach and I was sweating terribly but not sure why. Allison drove me to the dentist anyway and hoped the pain would subside after the appointment.

I arrived at the dentist's office eager to get this appointment over with so I could go home to rest. One of the dental assistants came in the waiting room to evaluate me and take my blood pressure. She immediately called the dentist over and he said I needed to go to the hospital—I was having a heart attack. I started panicking and sweating even more. At the ER, I was given an EKG, sent to a room, and placed under close supervision.

I spent the rest of the day getting stuck with needles from the nursing staff. Several different doctors came in and out of my room. After several hours, a doctor came in and explained that the heart attack symptoms were due to large blood clots in my lungs. I needed to stay in the hospital until the doctors figured out what caused the clotting.

Allison stayed by my side the whole time. She called Dad and his job to let them know what was going on. I was scared, and Allison held my hand and prayed with me regularly. I vowed to stop taking Phenibut as well as the pre-workout mixes. I also promised to stop drinking energy drinks. I knew that all those years of taking supplements in order to boost myself had come to an end.

The next week I still laid restless in the hospital. I was heavily medicated and depressed. Allison stayed by my side the entire time and faithfully encouraged me and lifted my spirits anyway she could. One evening I looked at her reading in one of the chairs and said, "You remind me of my mom. She would have cared for me the way you have. When I feel anxious, you gently hold my hand. When I feel exhausted, you kiss my forehead. I love you so much Allison. I thank God for bringing you to me every day."

I began to tear up because I knew this was another step in our relationship. I knew that she loved me, too, by the way she stuck by my side, took a week off of work to care for me, and slept in an uncomfortable hospital chair just to be with me.

When I was finally released from the hospital, I was given a series of medications for my heart and to help prevent any more blood clots. I tried hard to get acclimated to my new lifestyle without caffeine. I stopped taking Phenibut and all of the stimulants associated with boosting my energy levels. Now I woke up tired and stayed that way the entire day. I felt like I was fighting to walk against a current. It was a struggle to even move, and I knew going back to the restaurant was going to be a tough struggle for me.

I returned to work and found mass chaos throughout the restaurant during the opening. In most restaurants, there is a fifteen to twenty percent drop in employees from the time they are hired to the time the store runs efficiently. The Hagerstown location was quite the exception. The drop for this location was over fifty percent. The management team was frantically trying to hire new applicants and conduct training at the same time. Some team members walked around without knowing how to do their jobs. Chang placed significant pressure on the management team to work faster and more efficiently, which caused them to lash out at the servers. I was in a constant state of pain because of my heart and blood pressure, and the stress at work.

On New Year's Eve, I reached my boiling point. I was tired of fighting against everyone I talked to and had reached my end. Two separate times that night I felt sharp pains in my chest from stressful situations and that really scared me. I realized that if I continued this job I might have a heart attack or worse. I typed up a letter of resignation and left it along with my keys and managers card in the office for the opening manager to find. I was not going to jeopardize my life for a job that caused me so much stress and frustration.

The next morning, I received several phone calls from the manager on duty that day. I told them that I could not deal with all the stress of this job any longer. Primanti Brothers tried hard to get me to return, but I was not going to put myself in that kind of situation again. I told Allison about my decision and she was supportive. She knew the toll the job took on my health and agreed it was the best decision for me to leave.

OPENED DOOR

OVER THE NEXT FEW WEEKS I fervently read the Bible and realized a huge truth: everyone has been given the opportunity to receive salvation through Christ's work on the cross. Although salvation has been freely given to all who received Christ, the way to destruction is broad. Many people do not accept Christ because they do not feel worthy of Christ's love. I had always struggled with accepting help from others because I had never felt worthy of other people's love. I let myself think I could love others without truly loving myself.

I thought back to my time in LA when I learned some truths from Joshua. I thought that many Christians do not know how to accept love from others because they were raised in churches that taught forms of legalism. In churches plagued with legalism, if a guest who walks in with the "wrong" outfit, uses a certain Bible translation, or does not have the same theology as the other members, that person would be shunned by the church. I spent most of my youth thinking that this works-based faith was vital to a proper Christian life. I instantly thought of the sins I committed and felt unworthy of love from God and other Christians. Yet these types of people, who correct others without love or who cling to morality instead of the cross, are referred to as hypocrites and Pharisees in Scripture. These Christians constantly upset Christ in His ministry for their prideful and arrogant attitude to those who struggled. I saw that type of pride and arrogance at Mercy Academy when I was younger. I remembered how I was shunned from the church when I struggled with alcohol and partying. I constantly felt unworthy of love from others. I had no love for myself because I, like the Pharisees in the Bible, carried this judgmental attitude. I judged myself for my faults and sins.

I remembered the decision I made to forgive those who wronged me in my life. I realized the person I needed to forgive first was myself. I was finally honest with myself and asked God through prayer to give me full forgiveness of my judgement. I wanted to experience the gift of receiving grace from God, my Heavenly Father, and to experience the gift of receiving grace from others.

Through this realization, I found an accurate love for myself. I saw myself not for my failures and bad decisions, but as Christ saw me. Through Christ's work on the cross, God forgave me—I just had to believe that, too. I was no longer shackled by the bondage of resentment I had placed on myself for my past failures. I experienced freedom for the first time in my life. True freedom from guilt, anger, hatred, and self-loathing. I no longer fought against the currents of this world because I was free from the sin I carried for so long. Being free from my guilt caused me to give up the fight I had with myself, and to receive the peace that passes all understanding as the Bible promised.

I received a call for an interview with a grocery store about a mile from where I lived. I was not happy at the thought of bagging groceries, but I needed a job to keep me busy.

I started in a week, but first I needed to meet with my cardiologist. The doctor told me about a procedure that could be done to get my heart back in rhythm. If it was successful, I could stop my medications as long as I visited the cardiologist every four months. During the electrical cardioversion procedure, the doctor would basically stop and restart my heart. The procedure was generally successful, and my heart would be put back into rhythm. There was a chance, though, that my heart would remain out of rhythm even after the procedure was complete. Since there was an open appointment later in the week, I could start my job with my heart in rhythm with no medication.

I was excited as the nurses prepped me for the procedure, but also nervous since I would be knocked out completely. I briefly saw the cardiologist but I was asleep within seconds. When I woke up, Allison was holding my hand. The smile on her face told me that the procedure was a success. She reached over and kissed me on my forehead. The doctor told me I was no longer going to have to take medications and I would be able to enjoy my life again.

I did well at work, made good money, and was able to save since I didn't have to worry about rent. On my birthday, Allison took me to Gettysburg to sightsee and shop. We went to outlets in Gettysburg, and eventually came across a jewelry store. I held Allison tight and asked her if we could go in together. We walked in and looked through dozens of rings, but nothing stood out to me. Finally, I saw the perfect ring. I showed it to Allison and she absolutely loved it. I decided to have the store hold the ring and would make payments on it. I diligently made those payments, and I managed to pay the ring off quickly. Now it was just a matter of asking Allison's father for her hand in marriage. I knew this was going to be hard.

Thanksgiving came, and Allison and I continued the tradition of going to her parents' house for lunch and dinner. As we were getting out of the car, Allison joked about me asking her father. I thought this was a terrible idea. I was already nervous about asking her father, but I knew her brother would be there, too. I was sure they could figure out how to dispose of a body if they needed to, so I was going to wait. Lunch was delicious, with stuffing balls and tender turkey. Next came the pumpkin pie and whipped cream. Allison was too full, so she went to the living room to play with her nephew and niece. I sat around the table with Allison's brother, his wife, and Allison's parents. After a few minutes of small talk, I felt the Lord urge me to ask her father. I asked her father if we could meet some day next week. Her dad thought that sounded good, so I left it at that. However, Allison's mom wisely and quickly said, "Well, both of you are here now, no time like the present!" She had a smirk on her face while she shuttled the rest of the family into the living room. Allison's mom knew what was about to happen, so she ran interference with Allison while I talked to her father.

I started by telling Allison's father that I loved Allison very much, and that she meant the world to me. I commented that even though things had not happened the way I had hoped, I wanted to spend the rest of my life with Allison. I asked for his permission to have Allison's hand in marriage. I also jokingly mentioned that I was nervous about this part more than the actual marriage because I knew her father was a gun maker and hunter. We both laughed at my insecurity. Allison's father was quiet for a moment, and I was more nervous than ever. If he had any objections to this marriage, surely he would tell me now. He finally spoke.

"Her mom and I would be thrilled to have you as part of our family, Dan," he said.

I inwardly rejoiced and was filled with praise. I figured that the hardest part of the engagement was over, and now all I had to do was figure out how to propose. Allison's father and I sat at the kitchen table talking and laughing together for the rest of the afternoon. That Thanksgiving was the best one I ever had.

I could not wait to propose and I was a hopeless romantic at heart. I remembered that when we visited McConnellsburg, Allison took me to the top of the mountain and told me it was her favorite spot in town. I knew that mountaintop should be where I proposed and all I needed to do now was plant an early seed to visit this spot without drawing suspicion. As we headed out of town one day, I mentioned that I wondered if we could see Christmas lights from the top of the mountain. I told Allison I wanted to go there one evening and check it out, just to see if the Christmas lights were visible from that spot. Allison thought I was crazy, but she knew that Christmas was my favorite time of year.

Several weeks went by, and it was only one week before Christmas. The local weather station called for snow the next day. I wanted to propose before Christmas so that we could make the announcement to both families. I also knew that if I waited too long, the snow could cause it to be too dangerous on the top of the mountain. When I got home from work, I mentioned to Allison that everyone had their Christmas lights on and I wanted to go to the top of the mountain and see if I could see the lights. It was freezing outside, and Allison thought I was crazy. I convinced her that bundling up in heavy warm clothes and going to see her favorite spot would be a romantic adventure. She hesitantly agreed. We both bundled up and I snuck the ring in my jacket pocket. Allison and I headed up to the top of the mountain and listened to Christmas music as we drove.

The outside temperature gauge on the vehicle read fourteen degrees. As we drove up the mountain, the gauge dropped lower and lower. When we reached the top, the temperature was in the single digits. I knew I had to do this right, but quickly so we didn't freeze to death. As soon as we walked outside, we were instantly greeted with a negative wind chill. After hiking to the top, we looked out at the town of McConnellsburg and saw no visible Christmas lights. The wind whipped around, and our faces burned with the cold, freezing air. It was literally bone chilling. I hugged Allison and held her tight to warm her up. I thought about getting on my knees at this point, but I worried that if I let her go the wind might blow Allison right off the mountain. It was too cold to even think, but I thought it was safer to propose at the bottom of the mountain.

Allison and I slowly and carefully walked down the mountain, and when we were almost to the car I tried to draw her attention elsewhere so I could get down on my knee and surprise her. I looked off in the woods and acted like I saw something moving and asked her what was out there. Instead, Allison thought that I saw a bear, so she grabbed onto me tight. I tried to get her to look off in the distance, but the more I tried the more scared Allison became. Finally, I grabbed her shoulders and faced her into the woods and quickly grabbed the ring box and dropped to my knee. She thought I was trying to trick and scare her, so she pushed me. When she realized why I was on my knee, she started to cry. The emotional spectrum a woman goes through once she realizes she is being proposed to is amazing, and Allison was no different. All at once she was terrified, upset, and then cried for joy.

"Yes, of course I will marry you!" she yelled.

We ran to the car and embraced in a loving hug. We both thanked God again for bringing us together.

We went the rest of the way down the mountain still in shock from the proposal and from the bone chilling temperatures. We decided to drive around town and look at the Christmas lights before we went home. We talked about the proposal, laughed at Allison's reaction, and enjoyed each other's company.

Once we arrived back at her house, I heard a motor coming up the driveway. It was Allison's parents coming for a surprise visit. Allison had a giant smile on her face that she could not hide. Her mother asked why she was so happy and Allison showed her the ring. Her mother cried and her father hugged me when he heard the good news. It was a joyous occasion, and that night we started to plan the wedding.

Allison and I were eager to get our wedding planned. The wedding was set for July 1, 2017, and it gave us about six months to plan. We made the joyous announcement at Christmas to both families, and everyone was so happy for us. Within a month, we had planned most of the details for our wedding. Allison went dress shopping and called me that evening thrilled that she found the perfect dress. I found tuxedos for Kevin, Jeff, Marcus, and Derrick, my groomsmen. Our wedding day quickly approached and Allison and I were excited to be joined together as one.

All the preparations were complete, and the wedding party spent the night before the wedding and rehearsal and putting the finishing touches on the banquet hall for the reception. I went home with Derrick and spent the night before the wedding with my groomsmen. Allison stayed at the house with her bridesmaids. That night, I sat around the table at Derrick's house and shared stories of my past with my closest friends. I called Allison to tell her I loved her and to make sure she was all right. I knew that all the preparations for the next day were stressful for her. I went to bed early that night and woke up ready to marry my best friend. I showered and cleaned myself up as nice as possible. I was the first one at the church and went to the basement to get ready and clear my mind. I sat alone and reflected on my life.

I had faced one obstacle after another. I knew that without my faith in the Lord, I would have been lost. When I was young, I depended on Mom for every one of my needs. Just when I was becoming an adult, though, I lost her. I wished in that moment that Mom was there to share this memory with me. I knew she was watching me from Heaven and was thankful for the man I was. I went away from the Lord for so many years and gave in to my own desires to live a lonely life away from God's will. Through every trial and temptation, God was with me the entire way. The Lord loved me still. I remembered the exact verse that brought me to salvation, "But God commendeth his love toward us, in that, while we were yet sinners, Christ died for us." God loved me in spite of all the years of rebellion. God loved me enough to send His only Son to die for me. That was the ultimate sacrifice, an illustration of true agape love, a sacrificial love.

I loved Allison with all my heart and would gladly give my life for her. I was thirty-five years old and always thought I would never find true love, but I found myself just hours away from marrying the woman God sent me. God took Mom, my best friend, home to be with Him. In God's infinite wisdom, I believe He did this to prepare me and to mature me as an adult. When I was finally ready to be loved by someone else, I found Allison through God's divine grace. God delivered me from a life of sorrow and regret, forgave me for my failures and mistakes, and gave me a new life full of hope and peace. God took me back into His fold, just as the rich father did with the prodigal son.

Soon the pastor came, followed by Derrick and my groomsmen. The basement was packed with my immediate family and wedding party. I heard the church filling up with guests but I was not nervous anymore since I was right where God wanted me. The organ played and the pastor led the groomsmen up the stairs to the front of the church. As I walked up the stairs, I was overcome with happiness when I saw so many friends and family that prayed for me over the years. They encouraged me through my struggles and it meant so much. I waited patiently as I watched the bridesmaids walk down the aisle. I saw Allison's nephew with a big grin as he walked with his sister down the aisle as the ring bear and flower girl. She tossed rose petals along the aisle as they made their way to the front of the church.

Soon the music faded and the doors in the back of the church closed. My heart pounded through my tuxedo as I was about to marry the woman God made especially for me. In that moment, I remembered Mom at the foot of my bed telling me I needed to pray for God to send me a special girl someday that loved me and loved the Lord. I watched in anticipation, but the feelings I tried to hide so hard during Mom's funeral came barreling out. The organ music rang and the entire church rose to their feet. The doors swung open and there stood God's gift. I instantly wept, and Derrick put his hand on my shoulder to comfort me. Allison slowly walked down the aisle with her father and I knew that this was the most gorgeous woman I had ever met, both inside and out. God had answered my lifelong prayer.

In the story of the prodigal son, the most disappointing character in the story was not the prodigal son, but the older brother. The older brother was faithful to his father and worked in the fields. When he saw that his father gave the fatted calf to his younger brother upon arrival after years of rebellion, he was upset and frustrated instead of overwhelmed with joy. He thought he had worked hard for his inheritance. The older son did not know how to receive grace freely and became upset when his brother received it so easily. The older son failed to realize that the only qualification for him to receive his inheritance was to simply be a child of the rich man.

I had felt the pain of both sons. I had walked away from the comfort and security of my Father, and when I returned to the Lord, I did not feel worthy of receiving my inheritance which was rightfully mine—His peace. Once I remembered that I was a child of God and part of God's family, I saw myself as God saw me. I was forgiven through Christ's work on the cross. Once I saw myself as Christ saw me, I was able to love myself as Christ loves me. Instead of fighting against the pull of drinking, partying, smoking and rebelling from God's will, I experienced freedom from the rushing tide. I no longer carried the chains and burdens of guilt from my past. With this freedom, I lost the desire to live a double life.

I now saw the world through Christ's lens. Instead of seeing actors and movie stars as happy and rich, I saw the pain in their heart and the emptiness in their lives. The clubs no longer had a lure of excitement for me since through my new lens, I saw the loneliness of those people. When I saw people smoke marijuana, I no longer saw them as cool and calm, but as the hallowed shells they became with a lack of energy or drive to live a full life. Through this new perspective, I saw the depression associated with drinking alcohol. I saw drinking as an escape from the heartache and disappointment in life instead of a means to live in comfort. When I watched television, I now saw Satan's tricks used in movies, shows, and advertising. I saw the real truths of the world. I lost my desire to live in this world without living fully in the will of my Father. I now had freedom to live in peace through Christ.

Allison stood next to me at the front of our small country church. We looked at each other with loving smiles as we read our vows. We cried together as the organist played Mom's favorite hymn, "It Is Well with My Soul." This prodigal son shared the same struggles as both of the brothers in the parable and came back to the tender embrace of his Father. I truly felt that it was well with my soul.

EPILOGUE

THIS IS THE STORY OF my life. My life was filled with moments full of bad decisions, terrible situations, and living many years away from God's will. I wanted to share my life with you so that you know you are not alone. I wrote this book in hopes that people who have similar spiritual battles within themselves could find hope that there is peace in the arms of our loving Heavenly Father.

Romans 3:23 says, "For all have sinned, and come short of the glory of God." We all struggle with sin, whether it is outward and easily recognized, or inward sins that we hide from others in fear of judgement. We all fall short of God's perfection. Romans 6:23 states, "For the wages of sin is death; but the gift of God is eternal life through Jesus Christ our Lord." When we work, we get paid according to how well we did our job. The payment due for our sins is death and separation of God. Heaven is the sinless, perfect dwelling place of a sinless, perfect God. Our sin separates us from God. The most important word in that verse is "but." In the case of Romans 6:23, it starts out rather morbid, but there is hope attached. We are all separated from God because of our sin. But God sent us His only Son as a gift for us. Through Christ's redemptive work on the cross, our sins are forgiven. First Corinthians 15:3-4 says, "Christ died for our sins according to the scriptures; and that he was buried, and that he rose again the third day according to the scriptures." Christ lived a holy and pure life on this Earth. Then, He was willingly beaten and nailed to a cross and died. He was buried and three days later He rose again from the dead.

John 1:12 states, "But as many as received him, to them gave he power to become the sons of God." If we receive the "gift" that God gave us, God invites us to be forever part of His family. One thing I did not understand through my lifetime was the concept of eternal security. This verse changed my understanding. I was born a Burkhart, and no matter what happens to me I am always going to be part of my family. Once I accepted the truth that the only way I can get to heaven is through Christ, I became part of God's family, immediately and forever.

If you are not a Christian, let me share with you what Mom told everyone she talked with. "Today is the day of salvation," she would say. "Don't put off this life-changing decision any longer. All you need to do is admit that you are a sinner like the rest of us, believe in what Jesus did for you, and choose to receive the gift of salvation for yourself." My mom could not make that decision for me; I had to personally find my own faith in Christ. Pray a simple prayer and admit that you are a sinner and ask Christ to come into your life today. Prayer is simply talking to Jesus, it is not reserved for only pastors or priests. Talk to Him and make the decision to believe in Him today! Remember my story? Romans 5:8 says that "God commendeth his love toward us, in that, while we were yet sinners, Christ died for us." Don't wait until you are without sin in your life, because that day will never happen for you or me. We will always be sinners here on Earth. In the middle of stealing money from a business ATM, the lowest point in my life, I was loved by God. When I was at the club drinking, or at home smoking, God loved me enough to die for my sins. He loves you and wants you to accept Him as your personal Savior today!

If you have already accepted Christ as your Savior, then be a loving testimony to those around you. Don't be a Pharisee or hypocrite. Don't judge others for their outward sins or inward struggles. Love people where they are at. Christians have a bad name for our constant public judging of gay people, people who are struggling with divorce, people who are not married and yet living together, people who struggle with alcohol or drug abuse, or even our prejudices of other races or cultures. The Bible says, "Thou shalt love thy neighbor as thyself." We are a selfish society that makes constant excuses for our sinful actions. We take selfies, boast of our possessions on Facebook and Instagram, and secretly laugh to our friends or spouse when someone is dressed a certain way or acts a certain way that is different from our personal preferences. The Bible says, "Judge not, that ye be not judged." Shame on us as Christians for being such a sinful nation! We are told by God to love those around us and show love toward those that are hurting. Judging others is not our responsibility, instead we are to love those struggling around us.

Through my story you learned that I walked away from the Lord partly due to the prideful and arrogant attitude of many Christians. Let's make a decision today to love others, care for those in need, and reach out and think of others more than ourselves. I hated myself for years because I hated who I had become. Don't let Satan's lure of momentary satisfaction take away your joy. Instead, let your light shine bright!

The prodigal son went away from the safety and peace of his family. He let himself be drawn in to lustful desires and love of money, wealth, and fair-weather friends. Live your life with love, have compassion for those in need, and be a true friend to your companions. With much love and sincerity, thank you for reading my story. I hope it blessed you as much as it blessed me writing my story!

For more information about
Daniel Burkhart
and
Prodigal
please connect at:

@danburkhart50
www.facebook.com/dan.burkhart.10
danburkart50@yahoo.com

For more information about
AMBASSADOR INTERNATIONAL
please connect at:

www.ambassador-international.com
@AmbassadorIntl
www.facebook.com/AmbassadorIntl

If you enjoyed this book, please consider leaving us a review on Amazon, Goodreads, or our website.

More from Ambassador International

This spiritually-inspired memoir argues that, even during the worst of times, maintaining faith can ensure that our best days lie ahead. Victimization presents opportunity for victory, but with God all things are possible because He is the essence of faith.

From Victim to Victor: Walking By Faith and Not By Sight

by Dr. Deandre Collier

Five Minutes to Impact: The Final Flight of the Comanche is a true story of overcoming fear in the face of unexpected crisis, understanding the providence of God in the dealings of man, and renewing our faith in His divine plan for our lives.

Five Minutes to Impact

by David F. Osborne

One Step at a Time is a story of love, faith, family, and friendship, that shows that life isn't easy—it becomes what you make it. God truly can help anyone going through the worst case scenario, you just have to take it one step at a time.

One Step at a Time

by Brian Peahuff

www.ingramcontent.com/pod-product-compliance
Lightning Source LLC
Chambersburg PA
CBHW070049100426
42734CB00040B/2818